FORGIVING
YOUR
PARENTS

YOU *CAN* FORGIVE. EVEN IF:

- You were a victim of parental abuse, manipulation, cruelty, or disinterest

- They just loved you too much—smothered your individuality and kept you tied to home

- You still feel the sting of their accusations and blame

- You're overloaded with guilt and hostility

- You've had to deal with an odious stepparent, a long-distance parent, or a parent's untimely death

- You've already become a parent yourself—while still struggling with the anger and resentment of your own childhood

- Stop trying to forget: learn to forgive. And set yourself free. . . .

FORGIVING
YOUR
PARENTS

Robert Freeman Bent

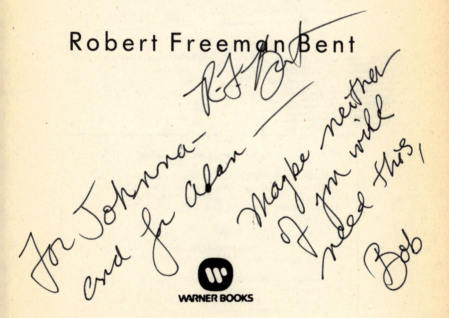

*For Johnna—
and for Alan

Maybe neither
of you will
need this,

Bob*

R.F. Bent

WARNER BOOKS

A Warner Communications Company

Warner Books, Inc., 666 Fifth Avenue, New York, NY 10103

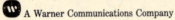 A Warner Communications Company

Design by Richard Oriolo
Cover design by Richard Milano

Printed in the United States of America

First Printing: August 1990

10 9 8 7 6 5 4 3 2 1

Library of Congress Cataloging-in-Publication Data

Bent, Robert Freeman.
    Forgiving your parents / by Robert Freeman Bent.
        p.   cm.
    ISBN 0-446-39142-5
    1. Parent and child. 2. Adult children—Psychology.
3. Intergenerational relations. 4. Forgiveness. I. Title.
HQ755.85.B46   1990
306.874—dc20   90-31497
                                                                CIP

For my parents,

Margaret Theresa Roach
and
Freeman Russell Bent

Children begin by loving their parents;
as they grow older they judge them;
sometimes, they forgive them.

–OSCAR WILDE, from the preface to
The Picture of Dorian Grey

Acknowledgments

The author would like to thank the following people for their encouragement and support: David Cross, Lis Harris, Don Madia, John O'Brien, Martin Quartararo, Selma Rayfiel, and a very special thanks to his agent, Susan Lipson, of Connie Clausen Associates.

Contents

PART THREE
THIRTY LESSONS FOR THIRTY DAYS

A Note to the Reader

If you have unresolved feelings of anger and resentment toward your parents, ask yourself the following questions:

1. Do I resent the way my mother or father treats me?
2. Do I feel obligated to visit my parents on holidays, even when I don't want to go?
3. Does my mother or father love me too much? or not enough?
4. Do I ever revert to being a child in front of my parents?
5. Even though my parents are no longer alive, do I still get angry whenever I think of them?
6. Is what my parents did to me unforgivable?

If you answered yes to any of the above questions, the pages that follow may serve as a helpful guide to resolving your anger. The ideas contained in this book are offered as possible choices, free of obligations. The decision to ignore or make those choices is up to you.

FOREWORD

Forgiving Your Parents is one individual's account of his search for a solution to the complex problems of releasing long-held resentments against his parents. His opinions are his own, but the concept of forgiveness can help all of us in our attempt to improve our relationships with our parents. This is an important book because it reminds us, in its simplicity, that change is possible even in relationships we gave up on years ago. By focusing on our parents' deficiencies, we overlook the fact that the capacity for change lies within us.

To talk of acceptance and forgiveness is not to underestimate the importance of the anger that children feel toward their parents. Good parents allow their children to separate, accepting them as individuals different from themselves. They know that the parent/child relationship is a changing one that evolves with each new phase of the child's development. In very much the same way, children can learn to understand and accept their parents by seeing their relationship to their parents as a changing one. Grown children may experience feelings of anger, disappointment, and hurt in relation to their parents, just as their parents may experience these feelings in relation to them. These feelings may relate to specific events in their lives or reflect a more general sense of being misunderstood, neglected, or abused. The act of seeing one's parents as real people, with strengths as well as limitations, is not dissimilar to other stages of development that the toddler and the adolescent experience as their view of the parent changes both in relation to themselves and in relation to the world. A grown child who is capable of accepting a parent's limitations is not so different from a six-year-old who is able to tolerate his father not being the "biggest," "strongest," "richest" man in the world, as he may have boasted to all his friends. The six-year-old may not be happy with this discovery, but he is usually able to tolerate it and continue his relationship with his parents, albeit with a changed image of who they really are.

Many people who become parents are ill-equipped for the job of parenting and lack the insight, motivation, or control to overcome their deficiencies. These parents may be acting out with their children the dramas or tyrannies acted out by their own parents. Or they may be going to the other extreme by reacting against their own histories. In addition, their energies may be absorbed by work, a destructive or unsatisfying relationship with a spouse, too many children, or countless physical, emotional, or economic problems. For whatever reason, many children emerge from the process of growing up with the feeling of having been abused or neglected by their parents. This can be true for children who grew up in two-parent, upper middle-class families as well as for children from economically deprived homes. The abuse or neglect may have been "overt," for example, beatings or abandonment, or may have been more subtle and "societally sanctioned," such as over-work by both parents or lack of interest and involvement in the details of the child's life.

The anger that an adult child feels toward his or her parents is frequently seen by the parents as a betrayal or a lack of gratitude. However, the anger of the adult child can also be viewed as facilitating the child's separation from his parents, just as it did in previous periods of separation/individuation such as toddlerhood and adolescence. This is not to say that the child's feelings and claims aren't legitimate: these feelings also serve a fuction in the developmental task of separation for the adult. By experiencing the anger, the adult is able to feel empowered in a relationship where he or she has always been the subordinate.

When a person examines and comes to understand what has actually occurred while growing up in his or her family, it is generally a painful process during which considerable anger is experienced. Robert Bent's book offers a possibility for change in how we view and experience our relationship with our parents. The purpose of *Forgiving Your Parents* is not to "cut off" these feelings of anger, which are essential. This book is intended rather for those who have been experiencing intense feelings of anger toward their parents for years and who feel "stuck" in these relationships. It is not meant as a substitute for professional help, especially for those who may have suffered sustained physical, sexual, or emotional abuse. But this book may act as a catalyst to those who wish for a more satisfying relationship with their parents, or who may feel that their anger is infecting the rest of their lives. For some people—after years of anger, whether expressed or unexpressed—this anger feels like their most powerful bond to their parents, as if fueling the relationship. There is often an unconscious fear that if the anger disappears, so will the sense of connection.

Some parent/child relationships never change. Fifty-year-old children may relate to their seventy-five-year-old parents just as they did when they were five and thirty, respectively. Sometimes this can operate in a harmonious way, based on the needs of the individuals involved. This is especially true in the case of children with strong dependency needs. Frequently, however, it cannot and leads to a loss of self-esteem for the grown child unable to assert him- or herself in the presence of the parent. This is often followed by depression and a sense of helplessness: "How can I be effective in the world if I cannot act like an adult in the presence of my parents?"

Many parent/child relationships do change. For many, this may be a gradual evolution based on the parent's "letting go," with increased respect and recognition of the child as an adult. For others, there may be a pivotal event, either in the child's life (financial independence, marriage, starting a family) or in the parent's (divorce, illness, death of a spouse). As children and parents get older, children may make fewer demands on their parents, just as their parents may begin to make more. All of these factors contribute to change in the parent/child relationship.

One event that seems to have a dramatic effect on the

parent/child relationship is the birth and development of a child's own child. Many grown children report that when they became parents they experienced a renewed surge of anger toward their parents. They often note that it suddenly became difficult to repress memories and feelings, previously thought resolved, when they were reliving (albeit now in the parental role) important early experiences. A frequent complaint is "Why couldn't they have done this for me?" Such feelings of anger are often followed by depression as new parents come to grips with the reality that their childhoods cannot be "undone" or "made over."

Another consequence of parenthood, although not as frequently expressed, is an understanding of and sometimes even appreciation for their parents. After the initial afterglow of the birth of a child, the recognition of the immensity of the child-rearing task often engenders greater acceptance of one's own parents. Seeing one's parents interact with one's child can be a powerful emotional experience on many levels.

It is important to remember that there is no "right" relationship one should have with one's parents nor a prescribed set of "healthy" feelings one should have toward them. Anger and resentment toward parents are common feelings. *Forgiving Your Parents* simply asks us to look at these relationships and feelings again, and reminds us that we all have a choice.

—Elizabeth Klein, Ph.D.

PREFACE

I was born to an unwed mother who gave me up for adoption at an early age, and my only recollection of my parents is memories of the couple who adopted me; my biological parents were never a memory or a factor. In other words, the absence of a biological connection did not significantly alter the familial connections I had with the mother and father who adopted me and raised me as their son. They were, and always will be, my parents. I had a typical childhood in most other respects, and the fact that I was adopted was simply that: a fact, not a problem.

I adored my mother and feared my father for as far back as I can remember. This fear turned into hatred and resentment as the years passed, aided and encouraged by my mother, who saw—and taught me to see—my father as "the enemy." She did this for her own reasons, and being a loving ally I followed her lead. In my household, the words "I'll tell your father when he gets home" were never uttered by my mother if I did something wrong. My fear did not stem from reprisals; it was simply endemic to the nature of our relationship. My father was an intruder, a man I saw through child's eyes as a towering villain capable of separating my mother from me. The fact that he rebelled against this (unfair) position with anger rather than tenderness only made matters worse. I saw him as a tyrant trying to assert his will over a helpless child and a vulnerable woman. I was much too young to understand the dynamic that was taking place between my parents; all I knew was what I felt: intense protection from my mother against the imposing presence of a perceived foe. The truth or falsity of this belief did not enter my mind at the time, and my father's attempts to reshape my image of him were destined to fail under the weight of so much maternal influence and power.

As I matured, my relationship with my father became more and more strained. The distance between us seemed unbridgeable, for him as well as for me. I followed his orders like a dutiful son, always aware that my mother would intercede if his demands became too harsh. In spite of his brute force, which was somewhat exaggerated by his physical strength, my father's manners were impeccable. It was the one thing I liked about him. We shared the same living quarters with little else in common, and his presence in the house was never less than foreboding as we circled each other like stray cats guarding our territories. My mother did nothing to ameliorate the schism between us; in fact, she seemed animated by our standoff, like a referee in a boxing match always ready to offer me the prize of her affections, which I seized with delight in the face of my father's inability to conceal his jealousy and disdain. From kindergarden through high school, I never once acknowledged a friendly request from my father without some degree of barely concealed contempt. If he expressed pride in something I had done (which was rare), I dismissed his interest until he forced me to listen. His disappointment in me was so intense that he fought my indifference with anger and hostility. Because I was young, and intent on pleasing my mother, I had no real knowledge of his pain and frustration; all I felt was his anger, and my main concern was to follow my mother's orders.

By the time I left home for college my father and I were barely on speaking terms, and I vowed never to live either with or near him again, a promise to myself that I did not break. After college, I moved to New York City and began a life apart from my family, with occasional visits home to see my mother. On these increasingly infrequent visits, I ignored my father as much as possible, giving in to his parental demands only to avoid creating a scene that might disturb whatever shaky harmony existed between him and my mother, a tenuous alliance that somehow managed to continue without the dubious connection that their only son had supplied. I was angry with my mother for her refusal to leave my father; her complaints were unceasing, and I resented her continuing to live in what I saw to be an unholy alliance. Because they stayed together for so long after I left home (although they eventually separated), I gave up trying to be both mediator and loving son to my mother. I also refused to conceal my contempt for my father; breaking away from the family home had instilled in me a false sense of courage built on youth, pretense, and the exuberance of freedom from what I then saw as the parental trap. Not quite a man, I took a stand of independence, which only served to alienate me from my father even further. And in doing so, I severed the bond—far more than I had anticipated I might—with my mother. Being a young man at the start of not only a new decade—the sixties—but also a new era, made me feel invincible. My parents belonged to the generation that those of us in our twenties were about to overthrow. In short, they were expendable, just like their morals and their political persuasions. I was hooked on the power of youth, addicted to a vision of a brave new world without the spectre of parental approval.

Ten years later both my parents were dead, my father surviving my mother by less than six months. Since I was still in my early thirties and without the benefit of brothers or sisters, the loss I felt was tremendous, especially with regard to my mother. The sixties were over, and I was alone. Any chance of a reconciliation with my father was obliterated by his untimely death, and I felt as if I had lost my only opportunity to find out what went wrong.

I struggled for years—both in and out of therapy—to understand the details of my personal history and why it had left me feeling consumed with resentment against a man I could no longer confront. My image of my mother, whom I had seen as a goddess in my youth, began to crumble. The slow, and often painful, process of forgiving my father brought a new dilemma: my mother as instigator of the problem. The more I began to strip away the layers of the past, the more difficult my problem seemed to be. If I forgave my father for his refusal to fight for my affection as a child, my mother automatically fell into a position of blame. Faced with the complexity of having to forgive both my parents—not to mention myself—left me burdened and perplexed. My stints with various psychologists helped to clear my perception of the past but at the same time seemed to exacerbate the situation for me; all they wanted to talk about was my childhood, and I felt the need for immediate direction in the present, a change of mind to help me cope with my life.

The guilt I felt for not coming to grips with the situation while my parents were still alive was more than debilitating; I felt totally unable to change both my circumstances and my future. Like most people, I felt I had no choice. And when that occurred, I felt powerless to make changes and succumbed to the grip of fear. It took quite some time—on my own, without therapy—to change my mind and regain the power I thought I had lost forever. My inner voice told me that I could learn to forgive, that the power of choice was not lost. I read everything I could find on the subject, enlisted the help of friends, and somehow managed to develop a system that worked for me in the process. This meant relearning some old truths that I had discarded along the way. It also meant forgiving myself and reviving my own self-esteem, my own sense of self-worth. I discovered that it is never too late to mend fences, to make peace with yourself, even if the person you need to forgive is no longer alive. Forgiving our parents does not depend upon their availability; it is the act itself that creates the possibility for change.

I began to notice slight alterations in my attitude one day when I inadvertently found a photograph of my father hidden away in a drawer. For years my lips had curled into a snarl at any sight of him. But as I picked up the picture I found myself looking into a mirror. To my great surprise, there was a smile in place of a scowl. I knew at that moment that I had begun to change, to alter my perception of my past. The look on my face provided me with ample evidence that being willing to forgive made me feel much better than holding on to the resentment I had carried into adulthood as if it were a relic to rely on, in spite of the fact that it had not served me well. I used this evidence as a starting point and followed a routine of daily exercises that helped to remind me I had a goal worth achieving.

By seeing my father—finally—as a unique individual who was also a "victim" of his own inadequacies as well as my mother's wrath and distrust, I gradually, but purposefully, began to forgive him. At the same time I knew it was essential that I forgive my mother for her role. We are all "victims" to one extent or another, and we all have a personal history to contend with. The fact that I did not have the opportunity to share my discovery with my parents does not lessen the importance of my learning to forgive. I have discovered that forgiving is something you do for yourself; a response, or lack of a response, is unimportant. The validity of my experience has changed my life for the better. For the last several years I have been able to face the future unencumbered by the baggage of resentment that I had pulled along behind me for so long. When I think of my parents—especially my father—my smile is contagious. In a sense, forgiveness has altered my memories of my childhood by illuminating what I had left in the dark.

Friends often ask me if I had any difficulty forgiving my biological parents for giving me up for adoption (perhaps the supreme act of love in many cases), and my answer is always the same. How could I *not* forgive the man and woman who gave me life and offered me the chance to find out for myself that as a member of the human race I have the right to be free to make my own decisions and choices within the framework of my experience? It is a right we are all capable of reserving for ourselves (with a little help and compassion), even in the face of abuse and oppression. To believe otherwise is to limit our humanity and our freedom.

In a book such as this, the question of the author's credentials tends to surface, since most self-help books seem to be written by those with a Ph.D. or M.D. after their name. My name appears with neither because I am not a doctor but a writer who has spent more than thirty years trying to forgive my parents for both the things they did and the things they did not do. Meaning that I was raised in a not-untypical family with a combination of affection, neglect, and abuse. And I use the word *abuse* to denote any and all forms of parental mistreatment, however minor or injurious that abuse may have been.

The pages that follow are the result of a careful analysis of those years and the process that helped me to embrace and understand the concept of forgiveness. To arrive at my conclusions, I spoke at length with friends and therapists and I entered analysis myself. I tried Freudian psychiatry, Jungian therapy, and gestalt psychology. I hit pillows to release my anger, screamed with primal force, floated alone in sensory deprivation tanks, spent fifteen arduous sessions connected to a biofeedback machine, and experimented with mescaline and LSD in the 1960s, when I was in my twenties. I saw psychics who read auras, palms, and tarot cards; learned

Yoga and proper breathing; ate nothing but macrobiotic food for one tiresome summer. I even immersed myself for a time in what is commonly called the New Age Movement, an umbrella-like label that includes a number of diverse groups, some with genuine concern and compassion for both the planet and its people, and some who masquerade under a banner of spirituality while they reject or ignore the reality of injustice and dismiss all accidents, illness, and victims as creations of the mind. I sifted whatever good I could find from what was available and purposely avoided channelers, cults, crystals, and cocaine. And I kept my distance from all religious organizations in an effort to defend my position that a belief, or lack of belief, in a higher power is absolutely personal.

In short, I tried, if not all, at least most of the therapies that were, and still are, popular and respected. I was looking for answers not just for myself but for those friends whose lives had become inextricably entwined with my own over a period of many, many years. I read voraciously, attended lectures, and listened to anyone who had something original to say about how to handle the unresolved hostility that affected anyone who had difficulty dealing with their parents. In the process, I made a simple, yet profound, discovery: I had the power of choice.

I rejected the notion that there was only one right answer, one indisputable path to follow. Therapy had helped me enormously in terms of understanding my feelings, but it was not until I opened my mind to the possibility of forgiveness—and made the decision to be willing to forgive—that I took the first step toward expanding my choices and taking responsibility for my own life.

I have since learned that unless we take that first step—a willingness to give forgiveness a try—we are mired in the trap of resentment and denial, unable to shed the constraints of the past. The friends with whom I shared my journey toward forgiveness added support, encouragement, and examples of success. Because I was a most determined advocate for change—in addition to being a writer—I found myself at the center of a diverse group of friends who shared both their difficulties and their small, but persistent, accomplishments. The bond that formed between us began to solidify after many years of starts, stops, regression, and progress. I was absolutely certain that I had found something worth pursuing and that if I did not make a change in the way I perceived my parents I was destined to repeat my past mistakes, with resentment as my constant companion.

The act of forgiving my parents seemed an impossible task at first, but it did not take nearly so long as I had anticipated. For me and others like me, making a decision to forgive was in some way a final resort. We had tried and failed after years of struggle on other paths, and nothing seemed to dissolve the anger we felt for our parents. In my case, therapy had given me some tools to use in my uphill struggle to overcome what I saw as parental abuse and indifference; it also helped to ameliorate my irrational fears and my tendency to fall into negative patterns of behavior. But it did not help me to forgive or to acknowledge the added benefit of forgiveness: the opportunity to change my mind and alter my perception without negating the truth of what had occurred in the past. It took me years to discover this on my own, but once I began to treat the act of forgiveness as a lesson to be practiced and learned, the knowledge that I had a choice became apparent and unshakable.

Knowing that it was in my power to make a choice gave me all the impetus I needed to move forward.

This book is the product of years spent listening, talking, searching, caring, and having the desire to point my life in a new direction unencumbered by the childhood resentments that threatened to stifle my growth and creativity. It is also intended as a helpful guide to others who are interested in the possibility of forgiveness as an alternative to anger, fear, and hatred.

My hope is that what I have learned will be of some minor—or even profound—help to those who read the following pages and practice the lessons offered. All the views expressed are my own interpretation of various human emotions with regard to parents. I make no claims that what I have to offer will work for everyone who reads these pages; I can only tell the reader what worked for me. Being able to forgive my parents has changed my life drastically; the old resentments that threatened to haunt me forever are now no more than a distant memory. Some of the friends who joined me in my search are included in the chapters on the various methods of parenting in Part Two, "Personal History." The names used are fictitious, the stories are composites, but the events are real, not imagined: they are offered in a spirit of empathy to help the reader identify with similar familial abuses that can be overcome through the process of forgiveness. One thing is certain: you have nothing to lose by reading this book except, perhaps, your resentment.

FORGIVENESS
DEFINED

Forgiveness is a pure act; it does not require a response. When you forgive someone you set that person free and also free yourself; this is the goal and the reward. To forgive is not necessarily to forget; it does not alter the past other than to change your perception of the past. By embracing the concept of forgiveness, you suspend judgment and awaken tolerance. If criminal abuse is involved and punishment may be required, forgiveness lets you leave that to those in a position of authority even if you are called upon to testify with honesty. Admitting that you were abused does not conflict with forgiveness because the truth is essential to real and lasting progress. To be a witness or victim of an injustice requires a response if justice is to be served, and choosing to forgive will not stand in the way of justice, it will complement it.

Forgiveness redefines self-interest by eliminating the feeling of separation from the world and those who share it with you. It erases the stigma of guilt and blame, it dissolves anger and resentment, and it does all this because it allows you to change your mind. The act of forgiving does not depend on any kind of religious, moral, or metaphysical beliefs; it works as well for atheists as it does for those who believe in a higher power. Forgiveness is a choice, a decision for change and growth, and a recognition that love is more vital to our lives than hate. In conjunction with forgiveness, love can be defined as an ability to embrace compassion and tolerance, allowing others the freedom to be themselves.

Forgiveness is the opposite of stagnation and confinement; it opens your life to choice and possibility and is available to everyone regardless of personal history. Above all, forgiveness is a first step toward defining who you really are in relation to the rest of the world, a world that includes your parents.

Forgiveness is not magic, even though there is an element of mystery surrounding what might, and often does, occur. In some respects, it could be viewed as a trick upon the mind. But it is a trick with a difference: it works without illusion. You may be so resistent to the concept of forgiveness that the only way to take the first and all-important step is to "trick" your mind into accepting the idea by pretending to forgive someone you resent. This could be seen as a "willingness" to give forgiveness a try, and although this approach is not as effective as the real thing, it is a beginning nonetheless. If by pretending to forgive you begin to feel a sense of release from anger and resentment, you may wish to take the next logical step and make that forgiveness real.

By understanding the nature of forgiveness—what it

means and how it can serve you—the action needed to make changes may be easier to summon. Embracing forgiveness requires action; it cannot be put into effect by remaining passive. That is why most of the excercises in this book ask you to speak aloud or to yourself; they disturb your comfort slightly and urge you to make a verbal commitment that is designed to alter the resentments that petrify your thinking. The lessons at the end of the book involve meditation-like action that allows your mind to become fluid rather than stagnant. None of the requests for action are physically demanding. Forgiveness is a gentle endeavor; the only sparring involved is that which you do with yourself. To draw blood is to miss the point. Forgiveness heals, it does not wound.

Forgiving Your Parents

PART ONE

PROBLEMS AND CIRCUMSTANCE

1

Introduction

This is a how-to book, a manual for survival in a world where fear and anger are too often the replacements for tolerance and compassion. Resentment against our parents is commonplace, even if those parents are no longer alive. Everyone who harbors an innate feeling that their parents were not good enough, not caring enough, or overly abusive, cannot help but benefit from learning how to release their anger and move forward toward a life that offers freedom from the resentments linked to childhood and the past. It matters little whether those parents live next door or a thousand miles away. Placing the blame on our parents for the failures we think we see in our own lives is the single most important factor in our misunderstanding of how to love. Our first exposure to love is with our parents, and when that powerful attachment is severely threatened, our ability to love is in jeopardy. It is the premise of this book that love— including love with detachment—is not possible without forgiveness.

Learning to forgive does not come easily to everyone, and in most cases it is something that must be accomplished with repeated practice. This book is not a substitute for professional therapy, but it could help those who are willing to change their minds about holding on to the anger they still feel—even as adults—toward their parents. We each have a personal history that can be sublimated but never truly forgotten. We are all victims of our past, and yet seeing the world through the eyes of a victim gives us limited vision, a distorted picture of reality. Releasing ourselves from this prison involves opening the mind to the possibility of forgiveness, an ordinary word used freely, but rarely understood or assimilated into daily life.

Resentment against our parents breeds guilt because all societies teach us to love, honor, and respect our parents, regardless of who they are or how they treat us. When we ignore the dictates of the world around us, in spite of verifiable justification for doing so, we often feel that we have done something wrong, that we are guilty of violating a basic family principle. And guilt is the fertilizer that hastens the growth of depression, anger, and irrational fear. It festers inside us, feeding on itself as it lashes out against our parents, then gradually begins to include anyone who reminds us of our parents before spreading to the world at large. To abolish guilt, we must rely on our ability to forgive and, by doing so, take responsibility for our own lives. Ridding ourselves of the notion of blame is another move forward, a giant step on the path toward freedom. Having a goal is also essential and something that each of us must define for ourselves in terms that make us comfortable.

There is no fixed path, no right or wrong. The concept of forgiveness can be seen as pure thought, unconnected to any and all religious or moral pronouncements. The fact that we are, as human beings, capable of forgiveness is not the question; this must be accepted as an irrefutable fact. What we are concerned with is our ability to make a choice, to open our minds to the possibility of change.

How you feel right now—at the present moment—will determine your success. If you are not willing to at least consider the possibility of forgiving your parents, no matter what they did or did not do, then the following pages may not have the desired effect. But if you can put your anger on hold for the short time it takes to read this book and leave yourself open to the idea that your mind can be changed and your perceptions altered, a chance for success is at hand. Ask yourself if it is worth taking such a chance. Only you can decide. We all tend to hold on to anything that is ours, including our fears and resentments. Letting go of destructive patterns is often more difficult than relying on them for misguided support. Negative emotions that are nurtured for very long periods of time can become "comfortable" and a means of defense against being hurt again, but once they are released a sense of peace fills the void, even if the process of release is painful. But the pain that is involved is in sharp contrast to the relief that follows when bad habits and unhealthy patterns are banished for good. When a defense is abandoned, vulnerability to pain is replaced with an open attitude toward growth and change.

Blaming our parents for instilling within us the patterns that cause us untold grief is regressive rather than progressive. We hang on tight to blame, unaware of the damage it is doing to our parents and, more importantly, to ourselves. By learning to forgive—and learning is the operative word here—we free ourselves from the past and begin to live in the present. For some, forgiveness will manifest itself by our letting our parents go and moving on to a life without them; in others, a reconciliation may occur, or a new sense of tolerance may surface. But whatever the outcome, forgiveness leads to the replacement of anger and fear with promise and hope. It steers us in a new and expansive direction and begins the process of healing.

This does not happen overnight. It takes time, patience, and effort. Opening a door that has been sealed for many years involves work, compassion, and commitment. It is worth the effort required, for beyond that door lies freedom. The key is in your hands.

2

Preparation

The first step to take is to admit that you have a problem with your parents. Almost everyone will readily admit to loving their parents, even a percentage of those who have been severely abused both physically and psychologically. When pressed for a reason for this love, the answer is inevitably the same: "I love them because they are my parents." It is as if a biological connection is enough to warrant a lifelong commitment to a love that seems required by decree. Yet the feelings adopted children often have for their foster parents proves that a genetic connection is not essential to forming an almost unbreakable bond; I am living proof of that since I loved my mother very much and might have loved my father if given half a chance as a child.

Biology is powerful, but it should not be construed as

a necessary ingredient for love. If it is, and the love falters, then guilt rises to the surface like a cork in water and floats through the relationship as a constant reminder that something is amiss. By loving our parents simply because they *are* our parents, we open ourselves not only to guilt but to an immense array of other problems, including sublimation of the truth. And when we live within the boundaries of a lie, we push truth beyond the perimeters of our experience and the honesty essential for a loving relationship is dissolved.

A great many people delude themselves into thinking that the problem can be solved by loving *one* parent and venting their anger on the other (I tried that and failed). By severing only half of their adoptive or biological connection, they think of themselves as a certified member of the family unit, able to love either a mother or father while denouncing the unloved half of the couple as a traitor to their union. The trouble with this approach is that it *seems* to work. It offers separation and connection all at once, and shifts the blame to a single focal point. All too often, the parent who is offered the love of a child joins forces with the bearer of the gift, forming a kind of partnership against the one who is regarded as unlovable. Shared guilt, although it is not recognized as such, has a way of disguising the reality of the situation by making it appear successful. But the unholy alliance of one parent and a child against the remaining parent is a certain prescription for disaster and long-term antagonism.

Being able to admit—alone, and without allies—that you do not unequivocally love one, or both, of your parents, is the first step in freeing yourself from the restrictions of the past. It is also a necessary step to take toward learning how to forgive. Telling the person involved that you do not love them is absolutely unnecessary. All you need to do is admit it to yourself, no matter how difficult that admission may be. By doing this privately, and without the need to hurt, you open the door to liberation. The truth *will* set you free so long as you accept the fact that it is *your* perception of the truth and no one else's. It need not be shared to be real. The validity of your decision to admit what you feel cannot possibly be enhanced by verbalizing your anger, unless you are fond of revenge—a worthless, degrading, and counterproductive emotion that engenders hate. Telling a parent you do not love him or her accomplishes nothing; it only makes your task more difficult. Keep this feeling to yourself—at least for now—and give yourself credit for being able to acknowledge the truth of your innermost feelings. Spend some time alone with this thought, and be aware that you are not alone. You are not the first person to have difficulty loving a parent, and you will not be the last. If you absolutely cannot handle your admission alone, share it with a friend but not with a member of your family. The time for that may or may not come.

If this approach seems harsh to you, remember that it is simply the first step. Learning to walk means taking one step at a time, and the same is true for learning to forgive. You cannot make progress if you ignore or hide your feelings, no matter how successfully or deeply you think they are buried. The truth always rises to the surface when you least expect it, and resentment against one's parents is a major psychological barrier to personal growth. Whenever young children do not get their own way, they are fond of telling their parents that they hate them. Wise parents accept this as a part of their child's growth, knowing that once the child has expressed his or her anger it is quickly forgotten. As we mature, we do not forget as easily; we take our grudges seriously and guard them as if they were jewels. But our deeply rooted resentments are not jewels; they are a kind of cancer that lives in darkness, terrified of the light of forgiveness. By learning how to shine that light directly on the cancer, we activate the power to dissolve it.

Take that first step now. Say to yourself:
I do not always love my . . .
(mother, father, parents).

Once you have done this, examine your feelings. Do you feel liberated or guilty? Was it easy to say, or difficult? Do you feel a sense of pleasure or pain for having verbalized your feelings?

Whatever your feelings are, acknowledge them. Do not attempt to ignore or hide them. Be aware that you have made a giant step in the right direction, regardless of how you feel at this moment.

Repeat your admission, this time out loud.
I do not always love my . . .
(mother, father, parents).

Tell yourself that what you are doing is necessary for *you*. By expressing your feelings privately, you have not hurt anyone, and no one is judging you. You have a right to both your privacy and your feelings, which do not concern anyone but you. Expressing the truth is another way of proclaiming your own self-worth and of recognizing that your feelings are your own.

**Look in a mirror and say:
I do not always love my . . .
(mother, father, parents).**

Was it easier this time, or more difficult? Remind your-self that what you have just done has caused no harm to anyone. No one was listening but you. This exercise is something that belongs to you and you alone. Cherish it as an active but nonviolent way to begin dealing with your anger and your fear. See this step as only a beginning, and open your mind and heart to change and growth. Be willing to forgive yourself for your feelings if they upset you in any way. Know that you have a choice, and view this first step as a positive move forward.

3

Trying to Please

We were not born to please; it is something we learn to do as a means of self-gratification during the years before we develop the ability to think for ourselves. Each of us enters the world with the instinctual feeling that we are the center of that world and everything and everyone revolves around us. This feeling changes for all of us as we mature, but not without training and the reality of disappointments. The world is full of adults who still believe that their needs and desires should be supplied by the world at large, and the pursuit of this course inevitably leads to an inability to function and mature. Infants have no regard whatever for their parents' comfort; they cry when they are hungry or want attention, no matter what time of day or night it might be. If they do not get immediate satisfaction for their demands, they scream until they do. This can be seen as the first form of verbal communication, and one that is difficult to ignore. If it is ignored, and the need for affection not acknowledged, the bond that is formed is faulty and may take years to repair.

As we grow older we learn that we cannot get what we want by voicing our demands loudly or unpleasantly. In short, we learn to please; we learn that by asking nicely we will get results more easily than by demanding. We come to understand that pleasing our parents is essential for our own well-being, since when they are happy we reap the rewards of peaceful coexistence. If we have parents who are difficult or even impossible to please, we face a startling dilemma: nothing we do seems good enough, and our self-worth withers. The reality that nothing we do will please our parents is a lesson so harsh that it is almost impossible to accept. There are those who spend their lives trying to please indifferent parents, with no apparent success; such behavior is degrading. Not being able to share our personal triumphs, no matter how minor they might be, is a cruel form of abuse that leaves the stigma of failure even when success proves our parents wrong. It often seems that no amount of praise from the outside world can replace or counteract the withholding of parental approval.

To combat this particular form of abuse, we must learn to trust in ourselves and relinquish the need for parental approval. If for years we have tried our best to please without success, it is time to make a change. The first step, as always, is to recognize the problem and admit that no amount of effort has worked, then we can choose either to try again or to abandon the effort completely. Choosing to abandon our efforts to please others will set us free without inflicting harm, but to make this choice without first forgiving our parents leaves us open to resentment and borders on revenge. By letting go of the past, with forgiveness as a guide, we can move forward with security and accept our parents as they are, knowing we can never change them because we can only change ourselves. And we must do this without expecting our parents to accept or understand that we have simply changed our minds.

Say to yourself:
I will no longer be obsessed with
pleasing my parents.
I will concentrate on pleasing myself
for a change.

We do not have to become a movie star or the president of a firm in order to feel successful. Success cannot be measured in these terms, despite what you may have been taught as a child. If you find joy in your work and create a life that pleases you, then approval from your parents should no longer be essential. To believe this without question and to feel the strength of this convictions in your heart are difficult tasks, but the difficulty should not hinder your effort to free yourself from the binds of parental disapproval. It can be done, even if it means severing your connection, although the opposite usually occurs. By making a change, and forgiving your parents from within, you may find that they respond to you in a more positive way, even though they are unable to fully explain the change to you or to themselves. This possibility is not a reason to forgive, since the act of forgiveness expects no reward but freedom: whatever the outcome of your forgiveness might be, everyone benefits.

The same standards apply if the situation is reversed: if your parents have never been able to please you. By forgiving them for what you perceive as their faults, and by forgiving yourself in the process, you can achieve freedom. By no longer expecting them to please you, you can alter the relationship in a positive way. If you truly have no respect for your parents—or for anyone else in your life, for that matter—try forgiving them and moving forward without them. You may lose contact, but you will no longer be consumed with resentment.

In some cases, resentment and anger may be the only ties left to your parents, and you may be afraid to sever these. This is a classic example of holding on to neurotic attachments simply because they are the only connection you can find. If you are terrified of releasing your anger because you are convinced that you will lose your connection to your parents in the process, try very hard to understand that anger provides no real sustenance or nourishment; negative emotions never do. See that you are fooling yourself with the fear of losing your parents. Honest affection can never thrive in an atmosphere of hostility. Forgiveness will dissolve your anger and change your perception of the bond that exists between you and your parents.

Look in a mirror and say:
I am no longer interested in
getting rewards from my parents.
Pleasing myself without harming others
is reward enough.

4

Victims

Modern science is rapidly discovering the role of the brain in determining the well-being of the rest of the body. This does not mean, however, that every single disease or accident can be controlled by our minds. The existence of lethal viruses is a verifiable fact, and drugs have been developed that have the power to cure a wide array of infections that no degree of mind control can match. This measure of scientific evidence has not discouraged a small but vocal minority from proclaiming that *all* disease is a creation of the mind and can be cured by simply adhering to a set of rules and following a system of beliefs.

On the other hand, studies have shown that certain diseases respond favorably—and can even go into remission—if the patient follows a healthy diet combined with positive thinking or some form of spiritual awareness. These cases are rare and scientifically unprovable, but they do seem to occur. The mind has been shown to have the capability to ward off colds, to make warts disappear, to stop headaches, and, conversely, to cause herpes. There is no evidence, however, that the mind can stop a falling brick from landing on someone who happens to be standing in its path. Nor can a mind nourish a body that is born in a country plagued with famine. It is also impossible to prove that humans choose their parents or that reincarnation occurs. The premise of this book is that birth is a biological phenomenon, not a choice, and that accidents and disease affect people at random, not because of a victim's unconscious desire for punishment.

Children are not born with an unconscious need for abuse; they need nourishment and affection, not punishment. This does not diminish as infancy gives way to childhood and adolescence, and if affection is either withheld or replaced by any degree of abuse, the person who emerges is often recognized as a victim. When that label becomes accepted as the truth, the search for an antidote that will alter or remove the stigma of victimization becomes labyrinthine. To believe that you are a helpless victim is to negate the power of your mind. Forgiveness has the power to point you in a new direction, away from the past and toward a more viable present; it is a choice you make for yourself.

Most adults who see themselves as victims—even if they are reluctant to admit it—spend their lives in the grip of fear. They are often unwilling to take chances, to leave a job they hate, or to share their feelings with the few, if any, people whom they trust. Thinking of yourself as a victim is a means of shutting out the world, since victims are rarely aware of the support that exists around them. Their connection to their soul—meaning that hard-to-define place that exists between the outside world and the inner self—is so damaged that repair seems out of the question. Acknowledging the fact that everyone is a victim to varying degrees—even the parents who abuse—rarely offers more than temporary relief, although it is an important first step. By holding on to the notion that the world is out to get them, victims often depict themselves as outcasts with no place to hide.

Shedding the role of the victim begins by having the desire to change, to discover alternatives that allow for growth and expansion. To choose to change your life will not negate the past, it will simply move you in a different direction. If you are tired of living with the mind-set of a victim, you must first accept the fact that you still have a choice and that no amount of abuse can take that from you indefinitely. Think of some of the people you have either known or heard about who have made positive choices in the face of seemingly overwhelming odds. A marathon runner with only one leg, for example, or a blind composer who plays a variety of complicated musical instruments. It does not take much effort to unearth a plethora of individuals who have overcome physical and emotional scars to such an extent that they enrich our lives as well as their own. It is more than a test of strength or a will to thrive that pushes even the most disabled to reject the role of outcast. People who triumph over extreme adversity do not live their lives as victims; they move away from the past and embrace the choices available in the present. Limitations are often denied or debunked, and failure is dismissed as irrelevant to those who acknowledge choice.

**Say to yourself:
I will no longer believe
that I am a victim without choice.
Countless others have paved the way for
me to make a change.**

Justice is not given at birth; injustice is a fact of life.
Victims of injustice fill the courts and the slums of the
world, but that does not mean that injustice cannot be
fought on both a personal and political level. If you are a
victim of parental abuse, no matter how minor it may
seem to others, and that fact has left you consumed with
resentment and unable to function without anger as your
guide, you might admit that it is time for a change. As
you probably already know, feeling helpless will get you
nowhere; even the act of forgiving requires your active
participation. It might help to acknowledge that you
have nothing to lose by trying, except perhaps your
anger and your fear. Many self-perceived victims use
their beliefs as a weapon in the battle with their parents;
without it, they feel disarmed. If you have been fighting
this battle for most of your life, you must realize that
victory is impossible for either side; the time has come to
call a truce by laying your weapon aside. Since all else
has failed, it might be worth the risk.

Forgiveness will help you to disarm yourself for the
simple reason that healing is included in the act of the
embrace. It ends the war, not with a promise of reconciliation, but with a guarantee that even separation is
better than unresolved hostility. If that frightens you,
consider the alternative: stagnation without reprieve.
And remember that forgiveness is a solitary act; it
involves no participation from anyone but yourself, and

the outcome is not irrevocable. By admitting that you no longer wish to be a victim, you avoid the trap of denial: the belief that what actually occurred in the past was an illusion. Forgiveness accepts the facts and moves forward into a new reality that rejects blame and guilt as irrelevant. It does all this by allowing us to change our minds and our perceptions.

**Look in a mirror and say:
I will not deny my past, but
I am willing to change my perception.
Forgiveness offers me a way
to change my mind.**

Getting stuck in the role of a victim can be temporary or permanent: the choice is yours to make. The time required to abandon the role depends upon how badly you were victimized and how willing you are to make a change. It can be very difficult for some people to relinquish a role that they think they were born to play, and there are those who refuse to change because a victim often receives more attention, mistakenly viewed as affection. Pity is not a healthy substitute for love, and self-pity is a poor replacement for self-esteem. Finding a suitable definition for love is as elusive as defining the meaning of life. The word itself is bandied about by everyone from corrupt politicians to bankrupt evangelists and self-proclaimed leaders of pseudo-religious movements with questionable intentions. Each of us must decide what love means to us personally, how it makes us feel both to give and to receive it. This decision can only be made when our vision is clear, and seeing the world through the eyes of a victim is like peering through dense fog: it limits, rather than expands, our view.

Forgiveness is expansive; it breaks down the barriers between apparent enemies and allows us to expand our sense of humanity. Being victimized is not the end of anything; it is an opportunity to make a choice. Rejecting the role of the victim and investigating the possibilities of forgiveness are two of the choices available.

5

Guilt

Guilt is a useless emotion, other than the fact that it allows us the opportunity to recognize how destructive our minds are capable of becoming. Understanding guilt affords us the chance to change and grow if we can banish it from our lives. Of the various emotions that we feel, guilt is perhaps the most negative and widespread; it wreaks havoc on our minds and bodies with all the power of an addictive drug.

Recognizing guilt is an elusive endeavor; it is such a powerful and evasive emotion that it can remain undetected until after the damage has been done. The all-important first step in removing guilt from our lives is to accept the fact that is it not an innate human characteristic. We are not born with guilt; it is something that is taught, then learned and assimilated. By recognizing that guilt is not an emotion common to all mankind, we can shed the belief that it is endemic to human nature. The only universal emotion may, in fact, be love.

Once you know that guilt is not something you were born with or that you inherited in your genes, you can then take steps to rid yourself of it with the knowledge that whatever has been learned can be unlearned, or clarified by further knowledge.

Say to yourself:
I was not born with guilt.
Guilt is something I was taught to feel, and
it can be relinquished.

There are three specific steps to dismantling the structure of guilt. We often take the first two steps unconsciously, but rarely the third. Taking all three steps is essential if guilt is to be understood and eliminated. For our purposes, each step should be done in private, using only your mind as the catalyst. No other action is required; it is something you do *with* and *for* yourself.

Step 1: Place the guilt on someone else.
Step 2: Take the guilt back upon yourself.
Step 3: Let the guilt go.

Step 1

When young children are playing together and something goes wrong, their first reaction—learned from the experience of an adult's disapproval—is to place the guilt on a playmate. When a parent or authority figure asks who made the error, the inevitable answer is "It wasn't my fault." Pointing the finger of guilt away from ourselves becomes a habit if we take responsibility only for actions that are destined to meet with approval and resist taking responsibility for those that are not. Children blame their brothers and sisters for everything that goes wrong in the household when they are not pointing the finger of guilt in their parents' direction. Taking responsibility for our own mistakes—as well as for our triumphs—is something that must be learned. To go through life believing that the world is at fault for not providing us with unlimited success is another example of detouring guilt away from ourselves. To consistently use the excuse that it is "not my fault" leads inevitably to a situation where guilt is placed where it does not belong. There may, of course, be times when a major or minor disaster disrupts your life through no fault of your own; when that happens, the concept of guilt is forgotten. But if your participation in some way caused the disaster, and you aim the guilt in another direction, you are denying responsibility by changing the facts. Repeated denials of this kind can only result in exacerbating the guilt by adding layer upon layer of accumulated guilt to an already overburdened mind.

The important thing to remember about this first step is that by placing the guilt on someone (or something) else, you can imagine that you are no longer the guilty party; you are "free" of the guilt even though your "freedom" relies on blame. Doing this—as an exercise only—allows you to proceed to the next step.

Step 2

Admit that you were wrong, remove the blame, and take the guilt back where you think it belongs: with you. Once you have accepted your own guilt you can examine it from a new perspective. Ask yourself if what you did was so bad and if your crime deserves punishment. Think of a situation when you placed the guilt on someone else, and try to remember exactly what happened. Reconstruct the details of time and place. Were you old enough or wise enough to think clearly? Did you do something you view as unforgivable? And if you did, can you now take the guilt and responsibility back upon yourself in order to take a closer look? Please do so, even if you find it difficult. You may define guilt quite simply as your feelings about something you think you did wrong.

How do you feel? Are you resisting the guilt? Remind yourself that the only way to eliminate guilt from your life is to bring it back to the source. Ask yourself how you could possibly let go of guilt if it is still placed apart from you. Tell yourself that this guilt is your creation and that it belongs to you and to no one else. If you feel a certain amount of sadness in accepting the guilt, recognize your feelings and do not try to deny them. Never feel ashamed or afraid to be sad. Be assured that by taking back the guilt you are in the process of setting both yourself and someone else free.

Say to yourself:
I accept my guilt as my
responsibility and my creation.
I now take back all the guilt
I placed on others.

Step 3

Now that you have embraced the guilt, you can decide what to do with it other than to place it back where it does not belong. Take time to make that choice and consider some alternatives. You can keep it with you for the rest of your life even though you realize it is the opposite of nourishment. Or you can release it into the atmosphere, where it cannot survive without a mind to harbor it. The choice is yours to make because guilt is your creation to do with whatever you please. Remind yourself that the whole point of taking the guilt away from someone else and bringing it back to yourself is to give you the power to destroy it. Can you think of any reason to keep the guilt? Will it serve some positive purpose or teach you something you do not know? Will it make you a more loving and compassionate person if you hold on to it? Or if you release it?

Walk around for a minute and feel the weight of your guilt on your mind and body. Are you comfortable? Is the burden too heavy? Sit down and try to relax. Is it possible to relax with the weight of all that guilt inside you? Imagine living with this guilt for the rest of the day, and then for the rest of your life. Is that acceptable? Close your eyes and feel the pressure within your head. Be aware that you have accepted this guilt as a conscious decision and you have the power to release it.

Say out loud:
I have the power to release this guilt forever.

Take a deep breath, and when you exhale, release your guilt little by little into the atmosphere, where it cannot survive without the shelter of a mind. Repeat the process over and over, and release more guilt each time you exhale. Do this until all the guilt is gone, then let yourself relax. Notice how much lighter you feel now that you have cleaned your mind of all that excess baggage. Be aware that by releasing your guilt you have set yourself and others free. Take pride in your decision, and be fully conscious that you have no regrets. If you had placed some guilt on your parents before taking it back upon yourself, recognize the fact that you have set them free even if you choose not to tell them. This whole ordeal has been a personal decision, a course of action for yourself.

Parental Demands

Part of what being an adult means is taking responsibility for your own life. Feeling responsible for your parents' welfare is a very special form of guilt. Having elderly parents who need your support is a common predicament. If you resent them for what they demand of you, and feel that your life is not your own, then steps must be taken to correct the situation. It is true that certain parents make unreasonable demands upon their children, and hang on to parental authority as if it were their lifeline to survival. In many cases, the breaking off of that familial connection may indeed threaten their survival, and that must be avoided. But if we cannot give our parents our love and support freely, and without guilt, then how is it possible to live a life of our own if we are at the mercy of their whims and demands, or even of supplying essential services that they often need? All traces of honesty are lost if we spend our lives taking care of parents we resent. It is a situation with enormous ramifications that requires some kind of a solution if we are to take advantage of the freedom life offers.

Abandoning parents who are unable to care for themselves is not the answer, although it is often perceived as the solution. Such action can only lead to an increase in our guilt, and a better solution can, and must, be found if we are to integrate freedom and joy into our lives. The truth is essential if we are to make a decision that does not harm either us or our parents. It is very important to remember that parents who make unreasonable demands upon adult children have lost the capacity to love and are relying on manipulation. It is also essential to admit that if we have no compassion for an incapacitated parent who has hurt us in the past, we are using our resentment as a form of revenge.

> **Say to yourself:**
> **I will not be manipulated**
> **by anyone, including my parents.**
> **Real love does not involve**
> **the taking of hostages.**

The key to solving this apparent nightmare lies in forgiveness. The ability to forgive yourself must be incorporated into any scenario that has a chance to succeed. Those who sacrifice their life for someone else because they feel guilty are living a life of dishonesty created by themselves. Caring for someone in need can only be done without guilt if that care is to be successful to any degree. An alliance based on resentment is counterproductive in every sense, and only forgiveness can ease your resentment and allow your parents to respond. If that response is more manipulation or a continued refusal to accept your right to freedom of choice, forgiveness will allow you to take whatever steps are necessary to make further choices.

Parents who refuse to acknowledge your right as a human being to be free can force you into what may seem like an inescapable corner. Remind yourself that you have the right to make a choice. Do not accept the false premise that no choices are available to you—or to them. Choice is the essence of freedom, and if that is abandoned, guilt is the result. Consider your options—no matter how inconceivable they may be at the time. They might include relying on professional assistance or government subsidies, or sharing your perceived duties with other members of the family, if there are any. Do not—under any condition—accept the notion that you and you alone are responsible for your parents' survival.

**Look in a mirror and say:
I have a choice, no matter how
difficult that may be.
My choice can be my
doorway to freedom.**

The feeling that you are trapped and that there is no exit from the grip of parental demands is an illusion you have allowed the outside world to manufacture with such precision that you accept it as fact. Your situation may be real, but your response to it is faulty if you think you have no choice. Freedom cannot be taken from an adult by demanding parents unless both parties agree that it can, even if that agreement has tacit support. Breaking that agreement involves your active participation, and forgiveness is a tool that can be used for a solution, but only if the forgiveness is honestly felt. The outcome of making this decision—to choose forgiveness over resentment—cannot be assured in a physical sense. A form of separation may occur even under dire circumstances. But blame and guilt will not prevail, and freedom will not be compromised.

Say out loud:
I approve of the way I am
handling this problem.
My time and affection is my own to
give, and I do so without guilt.
I will care for others while
caring for myself.

6

Blame

Blame is closely aligned with guilt; one cannot exist without the other, and they feed off each other like sharks in a ravenous frenzy. Both are destructive, negative, and useless reactions that are learned as children and taken for granted as adults. There is nothing natural or humanistic about these aberrations that distort our view of life. The possibility of removing the concept of blame from our minds is not only desirable, but essential if we are to acknowledge our right to be free.

Placing blame on our parents for what they did and did not do is as easy as breathing; it seems to come naturally and without premeditated thought. Puppies hang their heads in shame when they know they have made a mistake, while humans tend to blame anyone in sight rather than take responsibility for their own errors. We do this because we have been taught that we will be punished rather than forgiven whenever we make a mistake. It is an early lesson not easily forgotten, and the desire to place the blame on others tends to increase as we mature. Some parents and teachers seem to believe that punishment—rather than explanation—is the best way to correct mistakes, that without the threat of reprisal we would turn into uninhibited transgressors and offenders. And with this as our guide, we grow up thinking that guilt and blame are necessary for survival. Like most children who grew up in a volatile household, I blamed my parents for not providing a peaceful environment. The fact that they were miserable together did not alter my thinking as a child, since I wanted them to ignore their problem for my sake alone. I carried this anger into adulthood, until I was able to forgive and to understand the complexity of their dilemma.

For those of us raised in an atmosphere of blame, making a change takes effort if we are to unlearn mistaken lessons. The effort required, however, is simplicity itself, so long as you are able to abandon your skepticism and be willing to make a choice. Start by calling to mind people you may have known or read about—even religious and/or political leaders such as Martin Luther King—so that you can put a face on the concept. Having an example often helps to confirm the reality that blameless people exist among us. If one human being can make a choice to banish blame, then others can do the same. Forgiveness is again the key that allows us to see blame for what it is: a rejection of responsibility.

This is not to say that you are entirely responsible for every facet of your life; outside forces beyond your control are influential to varying degrees. But living with blame causes an ebb in the flow of life; it serves as a stopgap to growth and change. It is perfectly acceptable to acknowledge that big and small disasters occur through no fault of your own. But once that is accepted, forward movement should occur in place of retrogression or stagnation. Getting stuck in the mire of blame not only slows you down, it stops you from expanding your gifts and rights as a human being. And it might make you physically ill.

Say to yourself:
I have spent most of my
life accepting blame as normal.
I reject that assumption and open my
mind to another possibility.

Blame is not only directed toward others, it is also directed at ourselves. The litany of blame is often excessive and destructive in otherwise loving individuals. They blame themselves for not working harder, for drinking or eating to excess, for not exercising, and for not becoming a success. Or else they blame their parents for not doing enough, their friends for not caring enough, and the world for withholding support. In order to change this behavior, we must first forgive ourselves for all the things we think we do wrong. Forgiving others may seem easier to some, but real forgiveness is all-inclusive when it is done honestly: leaving yourself out creates a void that hinders success.

Try to remember a time when you had the feeling of unconditional love for someone or something. Perhaps you had a childhood friend or a pet that you accepted unconditionally in spite of faults or mistakes. If you have never been gripped by such a feeling, use your imagination to create the kind of love and affection that nothing can alter. If people pose a problem, concentrate on a real or imaginary dog or cat. Spend some time bringing the feeling of unconditional love into both your heart and mind. Accept the fact that a pet—and often a friend or a parent—loves you regardless of your looks, achievements, money, or ambitions; the love they have for you is unshakable. Use the power of your mind to transfer that affection back to yourself by forgiving yourself. Remember how easy it was to forgive someone or something that you loved unconditionally. Apply that same power of forgiveness unconditionally to yourself. Accept yourself for who you are—looks, weight, and mistakes included—and then free yourself from blame. It is nothing more than making a choice and reminding yourself that you have that right. Once you stop blaming yourself for all the things you thought you did wrong, it becomes easier to extend the same grace to others. Do not confuse taking responsibility with taking the blame; your only responsibility is to recognize that you are free to make choices.

Look in a mirror and say:
I refuse to continue to spend
my time looking for someone to blame.
I cannot change the mistakes of the past,
but I can replace blaming myself
with forgiving myself.

7

Negative Training

Children who are raised under the umbrella of negative training—meaning that their rights and emotions are subverted to the seemingly higher cause of conformity—are often expected to carry this torch of questionable tradition for the rest of their lives. The rules and methods of this training vary, but they invariably include the following: sex is dirty; success is measured by financial security; a neat appearance actually furthers this brand of success; any deviation from the norm is ground for dismissal.

Taking our parents at their word and discovering later in life that they have misled us, that their rules and regulations need not necessarily apply to us, infuses our minds with resentment for both them and their generation in general. It is imperative to replace negative training with positive ideals, and the first step is to recognize that our parents were simply carrying out the orders of their own personal history. The belief that money is the only barometer of success, for example, must be seen from an historical perspective. As common a view as it is, there will always be those among us who reject the notion and pursue other interests. In order to forge a path different from the one our parents followed, we must examine the beliefs that differentiate ourselves from the people who raised us. And once that is done, forgiveness will awaken our tolerance for beliefs we do not share.

There is no doubt that a child who grows up in a home where sex is discussed as if it were something to be ashamed of will develop a distorted picture of reality that can be carried into adulthood. Blaming our parents for that distortion is facile and unproductive. Steps can be taken to find our own truth so that the learning process can begin on a positive note. To most of us, this process is obviously more complicated than simply changing our minds. The sexual urge—to continue with the most blatant example of parental distortion—is one of the most powerful aspects of human existence. If that urge has been stifled, and confusion surrounds the expression of our sexuality, then blame and resentment run deep. Every emotion is ignited by sex: anger, fear, and guilt among them. To move forward unencumbered, we need to forgive what we often assume to be absolutely unforgivable. If we are unable to do so, we either risk our ability to function properly or carry the negative torch to the next generation.

Say to yourself:
The inability to forgive keeps
negative training alive.

Being able to make our own decisions involves knowing that we have a choice. Parents often raise their children with the dictum that they have no choice in a world controlled by fate or political bureaucrats. The inner life of the child is ignored in favor of conformity, and the nature of children is such that they rely on their parents ability to choose for them. (If they do not, they are strongly reminded just who is in charge.) But as we mature, we find that our inner voice is often different from the voices we have come to accept as unquestionably true. This poses a challenge as we continue to listen to our parents while making choices of our own.

Leaving home usually solves the immediate problem of making our own decisions, but the inner voice is consistently at odds with the memory of what we were taught as children. This struggle usually leads to anger and resentment against those who appear to have caused the inner feud. When this occurs, we stubbornly assert our right to our own opinions, and as we do this, we lash out at the parents who we think have stripped us of those rights.

Meeting our parents' resistance to the changes in our lives can be done with bitterness or understanding. Real forgiveness offers us the opportunity to truly listen to ourselves no matter how demanding or strident the voices from outside become. The ability to forgive can actually dissipate your parents' hostility to what they might see as unacceptable changes in you. And in extreme cases, forgiveness can offer you a way out by allowing you to let your parents go and to concentrate on your own priorities. If you do this honestly, with your inner strength intact, there can be no regrets.

**Look in a mirror and say:
I am an adult with a choice.
I can listen to my parents or I can
listen to myself.**

Seeing money as a measure of success is yet another parental and societal misconception that applies a kind of pressure to our lives. With such faulty training, we are rarely able to discern the real purpose of money without undertaking a complete overhaul of our financial concerns. For most people, money is a reward for working at a job that offers limited satisfaction. A more reasonable definition of success might be found if we insist upon listening to our inner voice instead of following the dictates of others. To toil at a job that is creative, whether it is painting a wall or a picture, assembling a car or designing one, falls under the concept of free choice. Finding joy in the making of money from work done with creativity is not an impossible task. Forgiveness opens our lives to uncharted territory by altering the effects of negative training. In addition, it alters our opinion of our talents and creativity to such an extent that by forgiving ourselves we free our minds for other possibilities, regardless of what we were taught to believe.

**Look in a mirror and say:
Money is essential for food and
shelter, but it is not
my way of measuring success.**

Conforming to our parents' well-intentioned dreams can be far more damaging than helpful. Try to accept the fact that your dreams may differ from theirs, but they are no less valid. If you believe in what you are doing and listen to your inner voice, you cannot fail—even if your parents see you as a failure. In making choices that satisfy your needs, your ability to forgive will flourish. Take pride in making decisions that are not intended to harm your parents in any way. Forgiving lets you turn away from the negative teachings of your past and create a curriculum filled with positive and life-affirming lessons, and the prospects for regret are nil.

8

Goals

Having a goal—or more accurately, a series of goals—often gives us the impetus needed to make positive changes without giving in to fear. Most of us resist change of any kind, preferring instead to continue our routines even when they threaten to strangle us. Fear of change poisons the atmosphere where dreams are realized and goals are achieved. The easiest way to hold ourselves back is to set our sights on monumental goals that are unreasonably demanding or almost impossible to achieve. One way to break this self-defeating cycle is to begin with achievable goals before moving on to more complicated endeavors. Goals that involve material or creative success are different in scope from those that are more abstract and personal, such as peace, acceptance, and understanding.

The first step is to differentiate between the goals your parents instilled in you as a child and those of your own devising. If you grew up in a home with less than perfect parents—as most of us did—you may wish to find a way to sever your ties to your past without upsetting the balance that connects you to your family. Your right to be intellectually independent should be a goal if that option has always been denied. Setting goals for fame, power, and money seem minor when compared to the real and achievable goal of being free to express who you are in both words and actions.

For example, if you have always wanted to express yourself artistically but were discouraged from anything remotely creative by parents obsessed with grooming you to become a business consultant, a real and achievable goal might be to ignore your training and study some form of art. Variations on this theme occur in millions of households, but those who break away from the fear of parental disapproval and reach for goals of their own are in the minority. That is why forgiving our parents for their transgressions should rank high on the list of goals worth achieving: it brings relief in the form of positive action and allows us to pursue our own dreams.

To live surrounded by the resentments and fears of the past is not only unproductive, it also drains our energy and diminishes our personal resources to the point where action is restrained or halted. How can we advance toward our goals if we are immobilized by fear? Or if we do break away without forgiving our parents, how much satisfaction will await us? To savor the joys of achievement, the absence of retribution must be absolute. Deluding ourselves into thinking that happiness can be found at the expense of others is a shallow victory at best. Real gratification comes to those who have left their anger behind when they reach a goal that can be shared.

Say to yourself:
My goals will be easier to achieve if I
allow myself room to forgive.

If your goals are concerned with exposing injustice, anger can be beneficial. A certain amount of credible indignation supplies the impetus required to sustain our energy. Hunting for escaped war criminals (to use an extreme example) takes enormous dedication and commitment to bring about an overdue conviction. Exposing someone who mistreats a helpless animal or child can also result in the restoration of justice. Both examples illustrate that difficult goals can be achieved by turning anger into a positive emotion for the sake of justice. It must be done with precision and care, however, if we are to avoid the trap of letting our anger destroy our inner lives. Again, this is where forgiveness can help, because it is something we do for ourselves. Anger laced with forgiveness is a powerful force in the battle against any kind of injustice. The combination works by defusing the irrational nature of the circumstance by a rational approach. Forgiveness does not change the facts or mitigate the need for punishment; it simply puts the task in a different perspective.

If your parents were guilty of criminal abuse or neglect, and your goal is to expose their crime, do it swiftly and legally. It may then be possible to forgive their actions without denying what happened. To forgive someone who has hurt you badly will free you from further abuse that you inflict upon yourself. Release

from outside abuse is a goal of sorts, but reaching that
goal while you are still imprisoned by resentment is only
a step, not a solution. Forgiveness gives you absolute
freedom; it dissolves resentment and allows you to move
forward without the stigma of abuse. By coming to
understand that you cannot change your parents' behavior, only your own, you enter a world of choice.

**Look in a mirror and say:
My anger may help me to expose an
injustice, but forgiveness will sustain
me by reminding me that freedom
is the ultimate goal.**

9

Becoming a Parent

The joy of becoming a parent mingles inevitably with other, more practical concerns about the best way to raise the new addition to the family. Memories of how we ourselves were brought up rise to the surface like warnings of a possible storm. Many new parents promise themselves that they will not make the same mistakes their parents made, that they will forge a new and improved method of modern parenting. Abuse of any kind is verboten, and methods of discipline become the topic of endless discussion. If we are too lenient, a sense of order in the household is completely lost. Forms of punishment become riddles to be solved with few clues to follow other than those supplied by others whose judgment is often suspect. Good intentions can turn into anger when we lose our tempers, which in turn awakens guilt. Every answer we thought we had can evaporate into thin air like the steam that warms the baby's bottle.

There is no perfect and all-encompassing solution that works for everyone, but if we forgive our children for their apparent flaws and forgive ourselves for our confused responses, our anger will dissipate and we will move toward compassion. Punishment can be replaced by careful, sometimes stern training, the essence of which is a reflection of our love. Preparing a child for what is generally regarded as the real world is always a reflection of our own perception of that world. If we view the world around us with forgiveness, our children will reflect our vision. A measure of control over the development of a child is implied by the parents' role, but our influence is never absolute. Each child is an individual with a unique approach to life, and by recognizing this fact, parents can allow their offspring to mature and develop at their own pace. Forgiveness offers us the chance to suspend judgment by accepting the various ways in which our children differ from us. When we accept these differences, we offer an expansive latitude of behavior by reducing our children's need to conform to some premeditated idea of how they should behave.

Parents who refuse to buy their young boys guns, for example, may discover that those same boys will fashion their own guns from sticks and brooms. To outlaw dolls from a growing boy, simply because we disapprove, can result in resentment of, or thievery from, a female playmate. Little girls who show an interest in baseball are often steered in the direction of a dollhouse or a kitchen and discouraged from pursuing sports. Denying our children the right to express themselves—no matter what direction that may take—is simply another form of abuse: a refusal to let them be who they really are.

Allowing freedom of choice is the gift that lasts a lifetime, and children who receive it have a better chance of succeeding at whatever they choose to do. Having a son who becomes a well-known designer of women's clothing, or a daughter who garners a position on a professional women's basketball team, should not be taken as a sign of parental failure. Any vocation that offers our children a measure of success and happiness is a scenario worthy of respect.

Say to yourself:
Compassion will temper my judgment,
and forgiveness will prevail.
I will teach my children that they
have freedom of choice.

Once we have made some major decisions about our roles as new parents, it is important to be consistent. Children feel safe with reliability and are comfortable with routine. This does not mean that spontaneity is lost, but rather that established patterns breed confidence and trust. Young minds adapt to changes in location much more easily than they do to changes in attitudes and routines. Bursts of anger from a normally tranquil parent are hazardous to a child's mental health, so if you find yourself steaming inside at something your child has done, remind yourself that forgiveness is an alternative to rage. If you are serious about not making the same mistakes your parents made, do not be alarmed if you find yourself repeating familiar patterns. We all rely on what we were taught as children at the times when we least expect to do so. If and when this occurs, try forgiving yourself instead; the example you set will be beneficial to your children. It is almost impossible to avoid making some of the same mistakes you think your parents made, no matter how well-intentioned those errors may have been. Having children of your own may make it easier to forgive your parents, since your understanding of the dynamic and enigma of parenting will become real, rather than imagined.

10

Obligations

The feeling that we owe our parents something, and are obligated to them for a variety of reasons, is strongly related to the feeling of guilt. If you are one of those people who has never considered the meaning of guilt, think of how you feel when family obligations demand your participation in spite of your resistance. These unwelcome obligations are simply one facet of a familial structure that comprises conflicting emotions, including varying degrees of guilt. Both essential and perceived obligations add fuel to an inferno that is fed by anger, resentment, guilt, and blame. When our parents are reluctant to accept us as adults with plans, dreams, and concerns of our own, they often expect us to fulfill the obligations they have devised, with little or no resistance. They lead us to believe that we have no choice, that parental obligations are a must. Under these conditions, you must recognize that choice is possible and freedom can be regained. One way to regain that freedom is by opening your mind to the possibility of forgiveness.

Holiday visits are a common obligation, to use an obvious example. To demand or cajole participation in a variety of national or familial celebrations such as birthdays, anniversaries, Christmas, or Thanksgiving might be seen as parental refusal to sever the umbilical cord. And the longer we adhere to these demands in direct opposition to our own desire to break loose, the more entrapped we become by the specter of resentment and guilt. The more concrete obligations incurred by infirm or financially bereft parents can cause even more bitterness if we begin to resent the seemingly inescapable predicament in which we are trapped. Forgiveness helps us to see that the trap is our own, a device created by our refusal to assert our true feelings to parents who we assume will either reject our honesty or resurrect our childhood fear of reprisal or even separation.

Say to yourself:
Unwelcome obligations are not
ironclad rules I must obey.
I am free to choose my own
response to my parents
demands.

If we elevate our obligations to paramount importance by playing the game according to our parents' rules, we increase our fears substantially. The longer this charade is carried out, the more difficult it is to abandon it before it destroys whatever real affection we might have left for our parents. Therefore it is essential to see this game of obligations and demands for what it really is: a circle of destruction that imprisons us within a barricade of negative emotion. One way to break down the barrier is to find the courage to forgive, and to rely on that courage to sustain us if we meet with staunch opposition. Real forgiveness dissolves the opposition by placing the power of choice back where it rightfully belongs: with you.

By choosing to forgive, we dissipate our fears and awaken our compassion. After that, the truth can be told without anger. If honesty leaves a scar, we must be prepared to console ourselves with the knowledge that the alternative is no longer an acceptable basis for a relationship. Living with the hostility generated by honoring obligations that make us feel as if we are reverting to childhood leaves us unable to deal rationally with any perceived authority figure.

Say out loud:
I am being unfair to both my parents and myself by refusing to evaluate my obligations honestly.

An obvious question needs to be examined: would it be easier simply to give in to our obligations to our parents rather than to assert our right to make a choice? Each of us must make that decision for ourself, keeping in mind the damage that acquiescense engenders. Bringing our fulfillment of obligations to an abrupt halt can appear as an act of aggression if it is not done with forgiveness. Forgiveness allows for gradual withdrawal and compromise—a better choice, perhaps, than an angry departure or acceptance of the status quo. Forgiving affords us an opportunity to preserve our integrity without negating the reality of our parents' needs.

Look in a mirror and say:
I cannot satisfy all parental demands without
jeopardizing my obligations to myself.

Minor obligations such as attending a traditional family meal or sticking to a rigid schedule of visits, letters, or telephone calls often become very important in the most average of families. Breaking the ritual is seen as traitorous by parents unwilling to acknowledge that their children have a right to make their own choices. Routine visits can eventually become stagnant unless all the participants are pleased with the arrangement. If you wish to make a change, you must remember that you are free to make a choice, even if it contradicts your parents' desires. You can express yourself with anger or compassion, and if the latter reproach meets with disapproval you can forgive and move forward. Remind yourself that forgiveness is contagious and often heals the deepest of wounds, so long as you are consistent. And remember that you cannot change your parents' opinions; you can only change your own. By making an honest choice, you also free your parents in the process. Families who know that their children are with them by choice have a better understanding of what it means to be connected by love and respect.

Say to yourself:
I have no desire to harm my parents.
I have the right to spend my time
free of obligations to a parent.

Those who are obliged to fulfill such major obligations to parents as the provision of money or medical care are faced with a more complicated response. Because we are often inherently grateful to our parents for bringing us into the world and caring for our needs as children, we may feel an obligation to return the favor. But guilt is never a good reason to do anything. Caring for someone you resent is damaging to both parties and creates an atmosphere of hostility rather than of healing. You may feel that you have no choice, but you always have a choice, no matter how difficult making it might seem. The circumstances of your dilemma may seem insurmountable, but if you are to survive as a loving, thinking, creative member of society you have an obligation to yourself to make an honest and compassionate decision.

If you make that decision with forgiveness as your guide, you cannot go wrong: forgiveness not only applies to others, it also applies to yourself. You may find that you are able to do things you never thought you could do. What was once seen as a disaster may turn into a source of positive change. Your humanity may surface after years of hibernation and reawaken your connection to the world around you. Whatever occurs, your ability to truly forgive will not let you down; it will heal scars in subtle and mysterious ways. And if one or both of your parents rejects your forgiveness or your offer of assistance to the best of your abilities, you can move ahead equipped with the knowledge that you have done your best, without the haunting specter of guilt.

Say softly to yourself:
I will do the best I can to help my parents
without ignoring my own needs.

PART TWO

PERSONAL HISTORY

11

Assessing the Past

We each have a personal history, from the day we were born to the present moment. No matter how similar our experience of life might be to another's, the experience can never be exactly the same. Our personal history is as unique as our fingerprints; no two people are completely alike, even identical twins, and we each perceive the world around us in direct relation to our personal history. We are the product of every single occurrence in our lives. We remember being hurt, and we remember being loved; we remember the smallest of details and often forget much bigger events. What we do with that incredible memory is largely a matter of choice and decision, unless we have been psychologically paralyzed by a trauma so extreme it cannot be overcome without professional help.

The chance that a book of this kind might cure the paralyzing effects of a childhood trauma of major proportions is minimal at best. Professional guidance should be sought for extreme cases of abuse, or by anyone whose life is in unrelenting turmoil. Finding good therapy is a task in itself, a task begun by making a decision to seek help. For those who need professional advice the task is worth whatever effort it takes. Dedicated licensed therapists and analysts are available worldwide, and financial assistance is offered to those who need it. Do not hesitate to take advantage of professional expertise if you are living with irrational fears and if daily functions are a problem. If you cannot find some joy in living, consider an alternative path and seek professional help.

But for the millions of others whose personal histories are a source of anger and regret, this book may offer some insight into the dilemma of living a life of resentment by holding on to a past that cannot be changed. Science has shown us that babies in both the human and animal kingdoms can die in infancy if love is not present. This means that if you have survived fairly intact and can function in a rational way no matter how deeply scarred you are, the chances are that you were loved on some level as a child. It is not difficult to convince ourselves that we were not loved by one or both of our parents, even if the truth is otherwise. Parents who do not love their children certainly exist, and it is important for you to make a distinction between common forms of discipline—or even minor (yet damaging) abuse—and real, not imagined, withholding of love. Abuse of children is widespread, and it manifests itself in a variety of ways. Each of us must decide to what extent the abuse that we suffered has shaped our perception of both our parents and the world around us.

Before we begin to embrace the concept of forgiveness, we must first examine the type and degree of parental abuse we believe occurred in our lives. It does not matter at this moment if what we feel is true or false, since it is our *perception* of the abuse that matters most if we are to disentangle fact from fiction.

Children tend to see themselves as the center of the universe, and especially as the center of their parent's world. Any and all denial of a child's wishes can be magnified into irrational proportions. The curious thing about adults is that even though we know better, we have a tendency to revert to childish behavior and thinking when it comes to a fair and honest evaluation of our parent's response to us when we actually *were* children. No matter how mature we are, we often act like children again in the presence of our parents. Our connection to them is so immense, and our memories so unforgettable, that we see our parents as authority figures for as long as they live, putting both them and us at a disadvantage. Taking responsibility for your own life is a way out of this dilemma, but this is easier to say than to do. Knowing that we have a choice is essential as well as helpful.

Say to yourself:
I am an adult who has a choice.
I no longer need my parents to make decisions for me.
I can take responsibility for my own life.

How accurate is your recollection of your personal history? Try to remember some good along with the bad. See your parents as individuals. Were they liked by others? Did they have friends, or did they rely solely on each other for company? Are they people you would have liked if they had not been your parents? Make an effort to be as honest as possible, and examine your past with as much detachment as you can muster. Above all, be truthful.

When you have finished answering these questions—and any others that may surface—try asking questions about yourself. Were you loving and giving as a child, or selfish and difficult? Were you grateful for what you received, or did you always ask for more? If you had brothers and sisters, were you jealous of them? Accept the fact that sibling rivalry can cause an upheaval in even the most loving of families and is often taken for granted. Give yourself the opportunity—alone, with no one judging—to make an honest appraisal of yourself as both child and adolescent. Were you the kind of child that you, as an adult, would want in your life?

The reason for these questions is not to place the blame on either you or your parents; it is simply an exercise in honesty, a look into your personal history, and an overview of your past. The pages that follow may offer some insight into what kind of parents you had. The categories, by nature, overlap. As you read, take note that incessant judging and intolerance (among other things) are forms of abuse that are as serious as the slap of a parent's hand. Abuse, like the temperature, is measured in degrees. Among the parenting examples offered, you may find one that approximates your own personal history. This may afford you the opportunity to consider a change in the way you view your past as it applies to your life today.

12

Strict Parents

Perhaps the most common of all abuses are those endured under parents who are overly strict. This form of parental behavior encompasses a wide range of restrictions: from not allowing makeup (for girls), to keeping the hair cut short (for boys); from never being trusted to go out on a date, to being sent to bed early for minor infractions of the rules. Everyone has their own list of restrictions that were imposed in their parents' home. Forced music lessons, required church attendance, not being allowed to drive the family car, time-consuming chores around the house, forbidden television or radio programs, dress codes, and disciplined hours of after-school study are just a few of the endless regulations that many of us had to endure. (Among my father's many requirements, he insisted that I get my hair cut every other week. Spending my childhood "scalped" no doubt contributed to my habit of wearing my hair shoulder-length throughout the sixties and seventies.)

When parental rules were not observed, punishment was often the result, and in many homes that punishment was harsh. Psychological retaliation against a child leaves emotional scars that last far longer than a reddened face or a welt on the buttocks. Many strict parents use physical abuse, an extreme and useless way to educate a child and one that is not easily forgotten or forgiven. Others use the silent treatment, shutting their children out of their lives for days at a time, forcing the child into isolation.

If your parents overburdened you with rules and resorted to some degree of punishment when those rules were broken, it is important for you to admit that you were abused. When confronted by hostile parents, children tend to assume that the fault is their own. The fact that you broke some rules does not mean that you necessarily deserved the punishment you received. Growing up in a strict household is a perfect breeding ground for latent hostility. The anger one feels at those who were harshly restrictive is potent indeed, especially since that anger could not be expressed without fear of reprisal. So we carry our anger into adulthood, siphoning it off in short bursts whenever the opportunity arises. We find ways of paying our parents back for the strictures they placed on us as children, doling out our revenge in bits and pieces like minute doses of poison designed to harm over a long period of time. We forget that the poison affects both the giver and the recipient, since one cannot expect to administer a potentially lethal dose without experiencing some sense of guilt, without paying an exorbitant price.

No matter what the degree of your punishment was, tell yourself now that you did not deserve it, even if you think you did. Try to remember that children are individuals learning to express themselves in ways that do not necessarily mirror their parents' behavior. Forget about blame for the moment, and simply acknowledge the fact that you may have been abused, even if that abuse was as minor as not being allowed to have a bicycle; after all, having a bicycle may have been the most important thing in your life at the time. Remind yourself that you were a child, with dreams and desires of your own. The fact that your parents were strict was not your fault, it was their decision.

Say to yourself:
My parents were overly strict, and
that is a form of abuse.

As you repeat this, do not concentrate on whatever anger may arise; simply state the sentence without judging. See in your mind the child that you once were, and close your eyes for a moment and comfort that image. Replace your anger at your parents with love for the child you once were.

Say out loud:
I was only a child who had no control
over my parents.
I saw their strictness as a lack of love.

If resentment against one or both parents enters your mind as you do this exercise, replace it with the knowledge that resentment is a cancer. See yourself as a child again, and imagine that child with the cancer. Know that you have the power to dissolve it with your love and understanding. Do it now. Take the cancer away from the child with your powerful imagination. See that child as he or she really was: innocent and full of love, as all children are. Concentrate on sending your love to the child you once were, and notice how good it feels. Understand that certain rules are essential for positive growth in a child. Accept the idea that you and your parents disagreed about the nature and observance of those rules.

Look in a mirror and say:
I may have been abused, but I survived.
In spite of my parent's strict rules,
I made it this far.

Be willing to open your mind to the possibility that although your parents were strict and you may have broken some rules, they loved you without knowing how to show it. Try to understand that the rules they imposed on you were a manifestation of their own shortcomings. Realize that whatever degree of abuse you received, there may have been some signs of love in your home. Dwell on any moment when you felt you were loved. Dig deep if you have to, but find just one instance when you felt some love from your parents, even if it seems superfluous. Put all other thoughts out of your mind, and see yourself as lovable, both now and as a child.

Say out loud:
I am capable of loving, and worthy
of being loved.

Repeat this until you are comfortable with the idea. Forget about your parents for now, and know that you are worth loving and always were. Sense the feeling of peace that this kind of thinking offers you, and understand that your mind is capable of calling up this feeling whenever you like. Recognize the power of your mind to make a choice about how you feel.

Joanna: A Profile

Joanna was born and raised in a small Midwestern town, and her family life revolved around the local Baptist church. Dancing was not allowed, makeup was forbidden, and all her extracurricular activities were connected to the programs offered by the church. She was unable to join her closest friends from school when classes were dismissed, since none of her friends were Baptists. Even in high school her dresses were baggy and plain, and her hair was worn in pigtails that were braided each week by her mother. When most of the members of her graduating class were out on dates or seeing movies and having a good time, Joanna was kept at home or confined to church suppers and family outings.

As a result of these restrictions, Joanna was treated as an outcast by her peers, who found her unattractive and uninteresting. By the time she left home for college she was socially inept, sexually unaware, and filled with anger about the way her parents had raised her. Since she was still financially dependent on her parents, she harnessed her resentment until her college education was complete. Once she had her degree, however, she retaliated with a passion: she moved out of the state where she was born, cut her hair in an outrageous style, and wore the most revealing clothes she could find. Since

Joanna was incapable of dealing with the opposite sex on almost every level, she offered her body to an array of men who used and abused her for years.

When I met Joanna she was in her early forties, still unattached but finally confronting the resentment she felt toward the parents she now saw only on major holidays. Since joining a women's self-help group she had come to understand that she was not alone in her feelings of inadequacy and was not the only woman in her group who had difficulty relating to men in anything but a sexual encounter. Her failed attempts at suicide had left her exhausted and vulnerable, but she was determined to make some positive changes in her life with the help of a therapist at the hospital where she had been taken after an overdose of sleeping pills. She gradually came to realize that her rebellion against her parents had done nothing to enhance the quality of her life, and the meager satisfaction she got from upsetting them did nothing to alleviate her inner turmoil.

Together we explored the possibility of forgiveness, and within a year—while she still paid weekly visits to her therapist—I began to notice a change. Then, after discontinuing her therapy and relying on the concept of forgiveness, she stopped going home for the holidays and visited her parents only when she felt the need to test her new approach. She told me that being with them was still nerve-racking, but less upsetting than it had been in the past when she viewed them as unforgivable. By dedicating herself to the diligent practice of forgiving the people who had caused her so much harm, she began to experience a sense of relief that was entirely personal and had nothing to do with the behavior of her parents.

When her father died, she felt an unexpected closeness to her bereaved mother, the primary focus of her former

scorn and outrage. By talking about her childhood disappointments and listening to a litany of the abuses her
mother had suffered as a child, Joanna was finally able to
forgive her mother and accept the woman's attachment
to the church without judgment. This act of forgiveness
did not increase her sporadic visits to her childhood
home, but whenever Joanna came back to New York
from a visit to the Midwest, it was evident to both of us
that the hostility and resentment had been replaced by a
new understanding and even a sense of humor. The last
time I saw her she told me that she had met a man with
whom she was able to communicate on more than a
sexual level and that they were thinking of living together.

13

Uncaring Parents

Some parents seem invisible: they are never around when we need them, nor are they available at crucial times in our development. Having parents who do not seem to care about the progress of our joys, sorrows, and concerns is more than frustrating—it instills and aggravates a deep-seated resentment that is very hard to overcome. Indifference is a type of abuse that is just as harmful as the various other types of parental abuses discussed in these pages, and it is one that needs to be examined.

Growing up in a home where one's presence is ignored leads to intense loneliness and depression, and often results in the need for professional counseling. Without the comfort of caring parents, children enter adulthood unable to trust, and when trust is denied, the ability to love is curtailed. Depending on parents to be there when we need them is not the same as compulsive dependency, which manifests itself as an irrational fear of being alone. Coming home to an often empty house, or to one in which we do not feel we belong, shatters our sense of self-worth, especially if it happens day after day and year after year. The memory of not feeling wanted destroys our self-esteem to such a degree that it takes an enormous effort to reassert ourselves, to have faith in our own capabilities, and to acknowledge the worth of our contributions to the world. In some cases, the need to excel is so great that it can be destructive—as if the only salvation were to be noticed, accepted, and adored.

This behavior is often apparent in criminals who seem prepared to do anything to be seen or heard, even engaging in heinous crimes for the sake of media recognition. They appear to relish the attention they receive. Others turn to money for power and notoriety; they search for acceptance or disdain, so long as it causes a stir. Behind the grab for success is a childish scream of fright, a desperate attempt for acknowledgment and love.

The awareness of one's self-worth is private and personal; there is no need to broadcast the news to anyone who will listen. Forgiving the parents who treated us indifferently is the first step away from the shadow of the past, where we felt unnoticed, where our dreams were told to unreceptive ears and uncaring hearts. Learning to forgive is a lesson we must learn for ourselves; we cannot continue to expect our parents to suddenly change and care about what matters most to us. We must do it solely for our own benefit, and in the process we will free ourselves from the need for parental approval by replacing that need with our own self-approval. Once we can accept ourselves as loving, caring individuals who long to share our love, we have made a move forward into a world composed of others who care. Forgiveness allows us to easily gravitate toward those who share our concerns, and that step moves us away from an uncaring past.

Say to yourself:
I am worthy of attention.
I give my trust freely to others, and
accept their trust in me.

Imagine that you are moving from a world of darkness into a world of light. Your parents belong to the world you are leaving. They have made their choice, as you now make yours. The fact that they are overly self-involved and indifferent to your needs is also left behind. Understand that the door is left open for them to follow, but you can no longer wait for them. Do not expect them to follow; simply accept them as they are, knowing that with or without them you are worthy of respect. This new world of light you are entering is inhabited by those who have chosen to abandon the need for their parents' approval and concern. They too have chosen to accept the fact that the past cannot be changed. In this light you are surrounded by people who care about your welfare, who are interested in what you have to offer. Open your heart to the trust of those around you, and know that your voice will be heard without shouting. Give yourself some time to acknowledge the changes that are taking place within and around you. Accept the truth of the situation: that your parents' behavior—in the past or in the present—can no longer stop you from feeling good about yourself and making progress at your own pace.

**Say out loud:
I cannot change the past or my
parent's indifference toward me.
I easily move forward into
a new world of caring.**

If you were abused by uncaring parents, it is important for you to remember that you do not have to cause trouble to be noticed. There are other, wiser ways to find the love and recognition you seek. You can recognize that shouting attracts attention, but it is rarely the kind of attention that can nurture. Emotions that are tangled must be calmly unwound, with a purpose in mind. Forgiveness calms the troubled mind and heart in such a way that years of conflicting emotions are able to find a new focus that is built on trust instead of fear. Since you have probably relied on anger to relieve the hostility you harbor against indifferent parents, you may also be aware that it has not helped put out the fire that rages within you. Remind yourself that you have a choice, that a new decision is worth making. Monitor the changes that you feel when you step away from your parents' world of darkness and enter a different world that you have created with your imagination. Stay in the light for a while and see how it feels, and trust in your ability to do this. Experiment with this exercise often, and before long you may find that going back into the darkness is out of the question.

If you really believe that you have no choice, that your uncaring parents have scarred you beyond repair, try pretending that you have a choice, even if you do not believe it. Do the exercise as if you *were* someone who has a choice. If you do this often enough, you may find that you no longer have to pretend, that in fact you do have a choice. You can change your mind about who you thought you were.

Douglas: A Profile

Among the many unforgettable things Douglas said to me was "My mother always let me know that she came first, and as a child, I wanted to come first in her life."

He also told me that it was not uncommon for his mother to serve him peanut butter sandwiches for dinner while she ate steak. If he questioned the meal, he was told that she was on a "special diet." By the time Douglas was ten years old, his mother had virtually abandoned him to the care of his incapable father. A year later she began divorce proceedings that sent Douglas bouncing back and forth between his separated parents in a custody battle that lasted more than two years. As a child, Douglas saw this battle as a form of love, with each parent apparently fighting over *him*. But as he matured, a truer picture emerged: his parents had used him as a tool in their unrelenting desire to wound each other without concern for his welfare.

When he left home at the age of sixteen—after living for years with his mother and her new husband—Douglas entered analysis. On his first visit home, his mother informed him that she had turned his bedroom into a den and thrown his belongings away. She allowed him to sleep in the den, and spent the weekend fawning over her new husband while she ignored her son's need for affection. Her attitude toward Douglas was one of complete indifference, and he resented her for it. He spent years in therapy trying to unravel the pieces of a family puzzle in which he seemed to have no place. His father had moved to another state without leaving an address, and no matter how hard he tried to get his mother to show some affection, her resistance was absolute. He would not stop trying, however, and the harder she resisted the more resentful he became.

I met Douglas when he moved to New York just after his twenty-first birthday, and during the first year we knew each other his mother left the East Coast for the West. But before leaving, she told him that his father had returned and was in a hospital for mentally disturbed adults not far from the city. Once a month Douglas would visit his father, but became despondent each time he did because his father could barely communicate. If he mentioned his visits to his mother on the phone, she would change the subject or bring the conversation to a halt. If he admitted that he missed her, she would turn silent and refuse to invite him to visit her new home.

During the second year of our friendship Douglas's father died, and he saw his mother for the first time in over a year at the funeral. She told him she had come to examine the will, which divided his father's minimal estate between them. A few months later, he heard from a relative that his mother would be visiting the East Coast for a few days, one of which happened to be his birthday. When the day arrived, he called the house only to be told that she was on her way to Europe and could not be disturbed.

Listening to Douglas made me realize how long and how hard he had tried to get his mother's attention with absolutely no success. We discussed his problem for years before he finally had to admit that nothing he could do would change his mother's indifferent attitude toward him. At the same time, his talent as a draftsman had begun to pay dividends, and the more successful he became, the better he felt about himself and his abilities. I introduced him to someone who offered him a raise and a position of respect. And although his self-esteem was rising, he was still morose whenever he discussed his mother's refusal to acknowledge and care for him.

Opening his mind to the concept of forgiveness did not come easily to Douglas, but when he was able to understand that it was something he needed to do for himself, his work improved and his monthly conversations with his mother no longer left him feeling bereft. He relished his new life and shared his good fortune with those who admired both him and his work. At thirty-five he was surrounded by a new family of friends and had stopped making his monthly pleas to his mother. He lost his desire to visit her, and called only when he got the urge. By accepting her for who she really was, and forgiving her in the process, he was able to let her go and free himself at the same time. We talked about the fact that forgiveness does not change the truth, it simply lets you view that truth from a different perspective. He recognized the fact that his mother was incapable of showing him any affection, and after years of being hurt, he was finally able to move his life in another direction by no longer demanding what he knew would be denied. He also saw that by focusing his love on a mother who was not receptive, he was keeping it away from those who were. By changing his mind and making a choice, Douglas released his affection toward those who could return it. And when that happened, his resentment dissolved.

14

Parents Who Fight

To children's ears, the sound of parents fighting is heartbreaking, a sound that remains even in silence. Children of parents who fight almost always assume—consciously or unconsciously—that they are the cause of the vociferous argument. When we are young we often take the blame for disharmony in the family because we see ourselves as the center of attention and believe that we alone are responsible for whatever battles occur. The fact that we were not necessarily the cause of the fights is difficult to admit—even as adults—and hanging on to blame makes us feel guilty. Then something strange occurs. In order to alleviate our guilt, we turn the tables around with a vengeance and place the blame squarely with our parents, overlooking the possibility that the arguments we witnessed or heard might not have been as serious as we imagined they were. By shifting the blame from us to them, we assume the role of victim, and this confuses the issue even more.

Most adults who spend a lot of time together disagree, often violently. Children are capable of both distorting the past and not being able to distinguish a vicious fight from an ordinary adult argument. All we remember are raised voices—and often slaps—that frightened us and disrupted our lives. As we mature, we feel the need for revenge upon the parents who shattered our peace and quiet, or we may feel retribution is deserved for a father who beat a mother.

This poses a dilemma: who was the guilty party? As adults, we are certain it was not us, even though we know that having children often causes stress in parents. What could have caused our parents to disregard our feelings by taking out their hostilities on each other? Why is it essential to have a guilty party? Was it mother's fault or father's? Can we ever know for sure what was going on between them? Did we not always take the side of the parent we loved most, even if they were the instigator? The whole process of placing blame leaves us confused. If one of our parents was intoxicated, we could blame the liquor instead of the person. But why did they drink to excess? Was it a disease? And if so, why did the other parent not seek help?

The dynamic that occurs between parents who fight leaves scars that cannot always easily be explained by placing the blame. As a result, we often render our judgment with as much hostility as they had when fighting. This response is not unlike a hateful tennis match, with the ball of blame being hit from one court to another. The best thing to do is call off the game due to a downpour of tangled emotions.

Say to yourself:
I am not to blame for my
parents' fights, and I never was.
The problems they had, or still have,
are between them.
Everyone has a choice,
and I am not responsible for
their decisions.

Even though you know intellectually that you were not to blame for your parents' fights, your emotions may not have caught up with your mind. See yourself as a child again. Know that a child is open to love from both parents and would not consciously try to come between them. Remind yourself that children want security and harmony above all else and would never instigate a fight between those who protect and love them. Even if you took sides, concentrate on the fact that you were only trying to protect yourself from further belligerence.

Say out loud:
I did not intentionally
try to come between my parents.
I was a child who needed protection
and love, not fights.

Now think about the tennis court, using the ball to symbolize blame. Hit it into the opposite court from yours with all the strength you have. See one, or both, of your parents as your opponent. Watch the ball of blame as it comes back over the net. Smash it back with all your might, only to see it return again to your side. See how foolish and boring this game is becoming. Imagine a downpour of freezing rain. Put down your racquet, walk away from the game, and find a warm and comfortable spot. Vow never to play the game again.

Say to yourself:
Placing the blame on someone is a waste of time, and I quit.

Notice how good it feels to stop the game. Any time you see the ball coming back into your court, just stand aside and let it go. Do this even if your parents are still fighting. See their game as just as foolish as your imaginary game was, even if they seem to be enjoying it on some level. Be aware that you are now mature enough to stop playing games that no longer interest you. Know that the game of blame brings nothing but suffering and pain, and it never stops unless someone refuses to play. Make that someone you.

Look in a mirror and say:
I absolutely refuse to play the game of blame.

If you find that you have carried your parents' battles into your adult life and tend to fight with someone you love, try to see the connection. Become aware that you are repeating a pattern, even as you recognize that when you argue you are not trying to hurt anyone who might overhear. Understand that many adults engage in loud and bitter arguments without being aware of how angry they sound. Tell yourself that disagreements can be solved in more loving ways, even though a verbal fight may occasionally happen without ruining the relationship. Open your mind to the possibility that your parents were not trying to hurt you when they fought. Accept the fact that they were caught in their own dilemma and chose to engage in battle, with you as an unwilling witness.

Say softly to yourself:
My parents probably did not know
that they had a choice.
Fighting was their way of
releasing their anger.

Caroline: A Profile

Caroline remembers burying her head in a pillow as a young child in order to muffle the sound of her parents' raised voices. But there was no real escape, and even when she was in high school she endured their early morning battles and their nightly arguments. At first she blamed her father for causing the trouble, but as she got older she saw her mother as the nagging instigator. If she tried to referee the skirmishes, she was told to mind her own business and go to her room. By the time she left home and moved into her own apartment, her resentment against her parents was so extreme that she avoided seeing them as much as she possibly could. She felt as if she had been cheated out of her childhood, so she lived in absolute calm. She rarely invited anyone to her new home because she was afraid that they would disturb her noiseless solitude, and she stayed on this path in spite of the fact that she was lonely.

In time she met and married an extremely shy and introverted man who never raised his voice. Together they had two children, and as hard as Caroline tried to be a loving mother, she could not tolerate the minor sibling rivalry that erupted between her two sons. She kept the boys apart as much as possible by dividing an average-size bedroom in half to keep them from fighting. This action brought a certain degree of quiet to her home, but her sons resented her for keeping them apart even though they professed to dislike each other intensely. It took years for her to realize that she had created unnecessary animosity—just for the sake of quiet—in what could have been a happier family.

Eventually seeing the connection between her own childhood fear of verbal hostility, she tried to solve her problem by attempting to dismantle her parents' marriage. She begged them to divorce as a way of ending their still-constant battles, which she witnessed whenever she visited her childhood home. She thought that if they separated, she could erase the sound of fighting from her mind, even though she rarely heard it up close. But her parents were determined to continue their battle and dismissed all suggestion of divorce or separation in a manner that helped to increase their daughter's confusion and resentment.

Caroline and I talked for years about her problem without making any headway, until we discovered the possibility of forgiveness. We both knew that the idea was not new or magical, and we accepted that. Caroline was determined to try anything that might alleviate the resentment that threatened to be passed on from her to her children. The boys were rapidly approaching adolescence, and she knew from experience that it was essential for them to feel comfortable at home so that they would not retreat to the streets of the city in order to feel free. Caroline threw herself into learning as much as she could about the concept of forgiveness as a way of changing her life.

Six months later we spoke about her progress, and she told me that her sons were more affectionate than they had been in years. By learning to forgive her parents and to accept them as they were, she was able to leave their house the instant they raised their voices. After a few aborted visits, her parents got the message and ceased arguing in her presence. Within a year she began inviting friends over for dinner and allowed her sons to do the same. The music they played annoyed her, but she accepted it as an essential part of growing up. There were times when she laughed loudly as she told me how she often sat alone in her bedroom with earplugs to block out the noise. She had found a way to tolerate their rivalry by accepting her sons as individuals. And they, in turn, had found a new respect for her, which they showed by keeping their adolescent battles to a minimum. Her husband found that he was able to express himself more readily in the atmosphere of understanding that Caroline's forgiveness had created. She became so involved in her own family life that her former concerns about her parents' battles were ignored if not entirely forgotten.

15

Uneducated Parents

Being raised in an environment with little or no intellectual stimulation stifles the curiosity, limits the imagination, and hinders the education of a child. Since education is not a prerequisite for having children, we often find ourselves with parents who can offer no help whatsoever in the development of our minds. Many of us have had to overcome a lack of parental help with school homework and the correct use of the language. Those who manage to increase their knowledge of the world with the help of early teachers often have great difficulty forgiving their parents for not providing a more advanced intellectual climate in which to grow, even when love was abundant. Since the acquisition of knowledge is rapidly increasing in the world around us, it is not surprising that the level of education in most families increases with each generation. Therefore it is not unusual for children to be far better educated than their parents. Most of us are aware that our thinking is not only different but more "advanced" than that of the generation who raised us. Cumulative knowledge has advanced, and the opportunities for education have increased.

Being resentful of uneducated parents is, in many ways, a form of egotistical superiority. A refusal to compassionately understand the histories of our parents' lives is totally unfair. Anger at those who never had the opportunity for personal advancement is quite different from anger at those who should know better. Accepting uneducated parents for who they are is an essential component in the process of forgiveness. Once again, we tend to think that we were the center of their lives and that they should have improved themselves for our benefit. But those with a limited education often have to work twice as hard to make enough money for food and shelter, and when that is the case, education comes last. Credit must be given to those parents who did the best they could under extreme duress and with little or no education of their own to help them along. Children can, and do, suffer if the household is run by parents who spend their lives trying to provide even the most basic of needs. However, to resent those parents for their lack of skills is unjust degradation.

If you are an adult who grew up feeling that your parents were not fit to raise children, you are entitled to both disappointment and regret. But if your feelings about the past are keeping you from acknowledging their limitations in the present, you are probably the one in need of forgiveness. Forget about what might have been, and move forward with the knowledge that you are able to make choices. Open your mind and your heart to not only your own family, but to all those who were denied the opportunity for an education. Know that being able to read, write, and speak correctly are not required to love well. Expand your vision and accept the fact that the world is changing rapidly. See the possibility that future generations may find your knowledge questionable or inadequate. Understand that your parents were not trained to raise a child and had to rely on themselves to make the rules. Remind yourself that even highly educated parents make terrible mistakes with their children, and the path to maturity is often riddled with problems.

Say to yourself:
Feelings are more important than education.
My parents had their own personal
histories to overcome.
They did the best they could
under the circumstances.

If your case is extreme, and you have difficulty reading, writing, or taking care of yourself, make a pledge to get some help. Let go of your past by forgiving your parents, and look to the future. Be aware that education is available to those who are willing to learn. Allow yourself the opportunity to be more than you think you are, and accept advice from all reliable sources. Do not be afraid to ask for help wherever it is available, and if you do not seek help, admit that you are making a choice to remain stuck.

Say out loud:
My parents had their own lives,
and I have mine.
I am willing to make a change.
I will ask for advice and accept
help with gratitude.

Paul: A Profile

Paul was bright, articulate, and good looking, but whenever he discussed his parents he always expressed his amazement that he had come from a family who could neither read nor write with any degree of proficiency. He spoke of them as if they were strangers, people who might have found him abandoned on their doorstep, rather than the loving family he occasionally admitted they were. He agreed that he was ashamed of them because of their lack of education and inability to communicate on anything other than a basic level. As a child he avoided bringing friends home, and that routine continued until he left home for college with a promise to himself never to return. Because they were poor, he worked his way through school with the help of a scholarship and a part-time job. During the summers, he found employment at various resorts that supplied both room and board. His visits home were infrequent, and each time he saw his family it took him days to recover from the shock. He was incapable of understanding the difference between who he had become and who his parents were.

Paul did not think of himself as abused, since his parents had never done anything consciously to hurt him. But he was consumed by guilt and a mixture of inferiority and superiority. He could not shake the feeling that he had never belonged in their care, and he vehemently refused to forgive them for not making an effort to improve their education and skills. Both his mother and father worked at menial jobs for minimum wage and lived on a very tight budget.

His wardrobe as a boy had been hand-me-downs from relatives and neighbors. When I met him, at the age of thirty, he was meticulously dressed and obsessed with his appearance. Initially I found him an unsympathetic character, a man who had chosen to ignore whatever sacrifices his parents had made in order to raise him as best they could. The fact that he had come from a loving, albeit uneducated, family seemed far less abusive than he was willing to admit.

Gradually, over a period of years, I began to understand his predicament and his failure to recognize that in most respects he had been blessed with parents who not only approved of him but were interested in his happiness. He began to understand his fastidiousness as a manifestation of his rigidity, and together we explored the nature of forgiveness. His guilt was so pervasive that he could not discuss his family without castigating himself for his behavior. His resentment was real, but his reasons were suspect to both of us. The anger he felt for his parents was actually anger directed at himself for not being able to accept his parents as they were. He acted like a man caught in a trap of his own devising: he could not forgive his family for what he saw as their ignorance, yet he was smart enough to know that his blaming them was unfair.

Paul's childhood wish was to have parents he could be proud of, and that dream did not evaporate with age. He had become a very successful lawyer and had offered to buy his parents a new home, which they refused, saying that they were happy where they were. He often suggested bringing them into New York City for a shopping spree without admitting to himself what he knew to be true: that a change of clothes would not alter their speech or behavior. Each time he spoke to them on the telephone he was overcome with disappointment at the way they mispronounced words and mangled the language. He told me that I was the only person to whom he had ever told the complete and unvarnished truth, and felt ashamed by that admission.

Learning to forgive his parents seemed almost incongruous to Paul, since they had never done anything to harm him. What he worked on was forgiving himself, and with patience and practice he succeeded. Three years after I met him he brought his parents into the city and introduced them to me. They spoke and dressed exactly as I had supposed they would, and Paul was relaxed and confident, with no need to be apologetic. He took them out to his favorite places and introduced them to everyone he met, telling me later how much they had enjoyed the city and how proud of them he had become. By forgiving himself for his mistakes, his childhood wish became a reality.

16

Parents
Who Disapprove

Growing up in an atmosphere where nothing you do is right, where approval is withheld at the times when you need it most, inevitably results in an individual whose self-esteem is in dire need of repair. It is almost impossible to have a sense of self-worth when your parents have never expressed any faith in your abilities. The anger that accumulates after years of being told that nothing you do is good enough is an anger of mammoth proportion. All children want the approval of their parents, both for what they do and who they are. If they are denied that, they often spend the rest of their lives feeling inadequate, unattractive, and unloved. Authority figures of all kinds—teachers, police officers, anyone in a position of power—pose an irrational threat to someone who feels that he or she is always doing something wrong. Creative endeavors are often ignored in place of menial jobs that are simple to perform, and real success seems always out of reach. When support is denied in a family unit, the child is likely to mature with a distorted and inaccurate opinion of his or her capabilities.

Putting a child's self-worth in jeopardy is certain to cause resentment later in life. If you are an adult who has never received the approval you think you deserve from your parents, then you are probably searching for that approval anywhere you can find it, in a desperate attempt to prove your worth. On the other hand, you may have given up the search because of a sense of imminent defeat, convinced that nothing you do will ever be good enough. You may have become an overachiever who spends every moment trying to prove to your parents that you can be highly successful and esteemed by others. However this denial of parental approval manifests itself, it should be apparent that nothing you could ever do will be good enough for parents who disapprove. The reason for this is simple: they do not approve of themselves, and unless they admit that, they will never be able to approve of you.

The most important thing for you to realize right now is that you cannot change your parents' beliefs; you can only change your own. If you can see that as the truth, you have just made a giant step in the right direction.

Say to yourself:
It was not my fault that my parents
withheld their approval.

Take some time to recognize that you were a child who did the best you could, even if you were not able to do things the way your parents wanted you to do them.

Perhaps you did not comb your hair to their specifications, did not play sports with the proper gusto, did not have a mechanical or musical mind, or were uncomfortable with the opposite sex. Maybe your mother or father did not think you were pretty or handsome enough, or thought that your hair was too curly or straight. It does not matter how insignificant the issue might have been; the need for parental approval applies to minor as well as major matters. Negative notions are not easily dislodged from our minds, especially if they are instilled in small doses by those who represent authority in our formative years.

Look in a mirror and say:
My parents were mistaken and I no longer
need their approval.

The fact that your parents may have set unreasonable standards for you as a child should not deter you from accomplishing what you want in the present. Many parents want their children to succeed at things they were incapable of doing themselves, and are afraid to admit to their own failures. "Stage mothers" are not a myth; they are all too real. Fathers who wanted to play professional sports instead of getting trapped in a factory or office are also an abundant species. Parents who disapprove of their children's ability to perform tasks often see their offspring as reflections of themselves, and any distortion of that image is looked upon as failure. This is a form of abuse and should be recognized as such.

Say out loud:
I do not have to live up to my
parents' irrational demands.
I am not a carbon copy, I
am a unique individual.

Through the eyes of a child, authority figures always seem more powerful than they really are, and seeking their approval is both natural and normal. However, continuing to want their approval as an adult is not natural; it is damaging and counterproductive. If we are absolutely certain that we approve of ourselves, no amount of disapproval can harm us. Confidence in our own abilities is something we must learn to cultivate, and one way to begin that process is to forgive ourselves for what we perceived as the mistakes of our past, for what we wrongly assumed were failures. Not having a talent for something our parents deemed important is not a crime, and to think of ourselves as failures is a mistake. Everyone must find his or her own talents and pursue them regardless of outside approval. Not possessing the physical attributes our parents may have wanted does not mean that others will not find us attractive. It is in our power to change our perception of ourselves by forgiving our parents for their own mistakes.

Say to yourself:
I do not need parental approval in
order to approve of myself.
If I approve of myself,
others will notice.

Children of disapproving parents often erect barriers to their own creativity because of the threat of failure. The creative process—no matter what form it may take—is something that must be explored. If something makes you happy, do it. Seeking approval for what you choose to create hinders the process and removes the joy. If you have always wanted to paint, for example, try to understand that your relationship with the work itself is what matters, and not the approval of others. To make our dreams come true we must be willing to experiment, to try things we have never done before. By learning to trust yourself—without fear of failure—you put to rest the disapproval of the past and move into uncharted territory. When you take that step, wave good-bye to your parents with forgiveness in your heart, and enjoy the journey you have chosen.

Lilly: A Profile

At forty-one years of age, Lilly is one of the most successful fashion illustrators in the business. She works at home in a studio that adjoins her spacious penthouse apartment; an elaborately planted terrace serves as her retreat from the pressures of her demanding job in New York. She has always been slightly overweight, but it does not detract from her inherent style and beauty. The clothes she wears and occasionally designs are a reflection of her life-style: elegant and comfortable. She lives alone, but has been dating the same man for many years; if the subject of marriage or children arises, she takes a defensive position. Her salary is more than double that of her constant companion, which is more of a problem for her than it is for him. Her mother and father live within easy driving distance but have only visited her apartment once; when they did they made it clear they were not impressed. They criticized everything about the place, in spite of the fact that it had been photographed by several leading design magazines.

Lilly's success has done nothing to ameliorate her parents' disapproval. In their eyes, she is simply an overweight, unmarried, middle-aged woman who spends her time drawing just as she did as a child. The fact that she is highly paid and admired for her talent is something her parents regard as another example of the excessive nature of city life. They constantly focus their attention on what they see as her failures: her lack of a husband and children, her inability to lose weight. Nothing Lilly had ever done was good enough for her parents, even when she was a child. As she matured she became terrified of marriage, even though she knew it would please them. Several years of therapy had made her aware that her fear of intimacy was immense and directly connected to her obsession with approval. But coming to that realization had not altered her behavior in either her professional or private life.

After her parents retired and were living on a fixed income, Lilly saw an opportunity to share the fruits of her success. All her offers for assistance were refused, however, and she finally resorted to buying gifts, which were opened, rejected, and stored in the family basement. Whenever she visited her childhood home she was treated as an unreliable child, and complaints about her hair, her dress, her weight, and her lack of feminine allure were common topics of discussion. With each visit or telephone call, Lilly was determined to get something from her parents—some sign of recognition, some form of acceptance and understanding—but her efforts were in vain. The harder she tried, the more distant her goal appeared. She felt as if she had spent her whole life trying to squeeze something positive from a family embedded in negativity.

The idea of forgiving her parents had never occurred to Lilly before I mentioned the possibility. Her resistance was strong, but together we explored the ramifications of such a drastic change of mind. Within six months after incorporating the practice of forgiveness into her life, she began to make some changes. She stopped sending gifts and limited her visits to holidays as a gesture to her new independence. When she did visit, she no longer stayed overnight in the bedroom that had remained unchanged since her teenage years. If her parents expressed rage at her new attitude, she either left the room or left the house, depending upon how irrational they were. The intimacy that was lacking with her lover began to increase slightly, but not enough for Lilly to accept his offer of marriage. Her new illustrations were considered the best she had ever done, eliciting praise from her peers. By forgiving her parents—and herself—Lilly discovered that her neurotic need for parental approval was something she could live without. She stopped buying the unappreciated gifts and ceased calling her parents to share her newfound sense of self-approval.

17

Departed Parents

The death of one or both of your parents does not necessarily mean the death of your resentments. In fact, it is often more difficult to forgive someone who is no longer a living target for your anger, and special attention should be paid to a situation where hostility exists toward someone who is no longer capable of a response. Living with the memory of abuse, in any form, from a mother or father who is not available for communication can leave one feeling frustrated, angry, and consumed with guilt. These feelings are magnified far more than they would be if that parent were still alive and retribution still an option. Finding yourself in this emotional bind may lead you to believe that there is no way out, but that is not the case. Forgiveness does not depend on being able to express it to someone other than yourself, and this is the essence of its success. Forgiveness is absolutely personal and pure; it can be accomplished whether or not the object of forgiveness is alive or dead.

Years after my parents had died I felt that I had lost forever the opportunity to forgive them, since a meeting was no longer possible. Yet, once I grasped the realization that forgiveness does not depend on a response in order to be effective, I proved to myself that it was true. The act of forgiving presented a special set of problems: I had the advantage of knowing my forgiveness could not be rejected, but I also had to accept the fact that I would spend the rest of my life without the opportunity to experience my forgiveness face-to-face. There were times when forgiving my parents seemed easier because they were no longer alive to witness my choice, but at times I firmly believed that a confrontation was essential. Many children of departed parents may share my initial confusion; this is perfectly understandable. Those whose parents are still alive may be under the mistaken impression that forgiveness is easier to embrace if one's parents are deceased. This book is a testament to my belief that forgiving your parents is something you do for yourself; the whereabouts of your parents is irrelevant.

Say to yourself:
It is not necessary for me to tell my
parents that I forgive them.
All that is essential is that I
trust my own convictions.

The act of forgiveness is something you do for yourself. A response to your forgiveness is irrelevant to the act itself. Since there can be no response from departed parents, the fact that you were unable to forgive them when they were alive is not something you have any power to change. What you can do is give yourself credit for having the wisdom to forgive them at all, and take some pride in your decision. The release you will feel should be enough to prove to you that the act alone is what is important. If you have truly forgiven your parents, no response is necessary.

Say out loud:
I cannot change the past.
Forgiveness does not require a response;
it is a personal choice.

If you have a parent who abandoned you, and whom you know is still alive but have no way of reaching, remind yourself again that forgiveness does not depend on your ability to discuss your decision with the person you have forgiven. If you spend any time at all thinking of tracking your missing parent down to vent your anger, consider forgiveness as an alternative that will have the power to dissolve the idea of a confrontation and set you free in the process. Finding a missing parent may offer some rewards, but revenge is not one of them, since revenge is never a positive move. Whatever you may have heard about the parent who abandoned you may or may not be the truth. Embracing the concept of forgiveness is a choice you make for yourself, not the missing person.

Look in a mirror and say:
Being abandoned does not mean
I must seek revenge.
I will consider forgiveness as an alternative.

It is very important for those without parents to remember that they are not alone in the world. We are, as human beings, interrelated. As we grow older, friends, lovers, children, or spouses become our new family. Getting stuck in the mire of thinking that we have been abandoned by parents who have disappeared, died, or moved away is a negative approach to reality. We cannot change what others do, but we can change ourselves. If you feel that you have been abandoned in any way, consider the possibility of moving away from the past and taking responsibility for the present. The act of forgiveness does not erase the past or hide the truth, but it does change your perception of that past in a way that allows progress to replace regression. It gives you the opportunity to release the past from your mind and concentrate more fully on the present, to focus your attention on what can be changed instead of what occurred.

If your parents have died and you feel the need to visit their burial site in order to verbalize your forgiveness, do so. A ritual such as this can often strengthen your resolve. But try to understand that forgiveness is internal and need not be shared. Remember this if you trace a missing parent just for the satisfaction of telling him or her that you have forgiven them. This is not a pure act; it smacks of revenge masquerading as kindness. Another way to deal with this kind of obsession is to write a letter that you never mail, telling the parent who is unavailable that you have forgiven them for all the terrible things you think that you endured. Write the letter with all the force and passion at your command, and list everything that the parent did to cause you pain. Spell out every detail of how you felt when he or she abused you in any way, including minor restrictions of any kind. Use whatever words come into your mind and fill each page with all the anger you feel. Then, when you have put your resentment in words, forgive your parent. Hide the letter in a safe place overnight and imagine the person receiving and reading it. When you awake, destroy the letter without thinking about it, knowing it has served a purpose by giving you an opportunity to release your anger.

John: A Profile

John's mother died of cancer after a yearlong battle with the disease; six months later his father passed away. John was thirty years old at the time and had no brothers, sisters, or relatives of any kind. His parents had separated a few years before their deaths, and John had remained close only to his mother. He was proud of her decision to leave the man who had abused them both for as long as he could remember. As a child, John was forced to work with his father after school while the other children in the neighborhood were free to pursue their own interests. His father would get drunk before dinner each evening, and spend the rest of the night arguing with John's mother, even after John went to bed. Listening to their raised voices would fill him with anger toward his father for causing the trouble, and toward his mother for not getting a divorce. The hatred he felt for his father was so intense that he often thought of killing him, even though he knew he could never commit such a crime. He imagined that his father might disappear, die in his sleep, or be kidnapped by assassins. But these macabre wishes never materialized.

When John left for college, his mother finally found the strength to leave her husband. John visited her often in her rented apartment, and their relationship flourished. Because he trusted his mother, John confessed to being a homosexual, but not before demanding and receiving a promise from her that she would never tell his father. His mother made some confessions of her own by telling her son that his father had never wanted to have children and that when John was born his father had disappeared for days on a drunken adventure. John listened to his mother's story convinced that his father was a man without a heart.

When his mother died a few years later, John gave in to outside pressure and met with his father concerning the funeral arrangements. They had not seen each other in almost five years, and his father was a changed man, obviously ill and stricken with grief. John had great difficulty believing that his father's remorse was genuine, and after the burial he never saw his father again.

I met John a few years after his father died; he was still visibly shaken whenever he talked about the man. He blamed his father for his mother's early death, for his own unhappiness, and for every unpleasant moment in his past. The possibility of forgiving the man he had hated for most of his life seemed remote at best. He expressed one regret: that he had not had the chance to tell his father that he was homosexual. He knew that the news would have wounded his father's image of masculinity, and he was furious for denying himself the opportunity to deliver a punch where he knew it would hurt his father most. He smiled as he imagined the look on his father's face if he had ever learned the truth.

The concept of forgiveness appealed to John for one reason only: he saw it as a way out of his obsession with the past. The fact that his reasoning was faulty did not stop me from encouraging him to consider the possibility.

As we talked, month after month, a curious thing happened: we discovered together that finding an apparently valid reason to forgive did not in any way hinder the act itself. John began to see his father as a deeply troubled alcoholic whose resources were buried by the disease. Over a period of approximately a year, John entered a new phase in his life by forgiving what he saw as his father's inability to discover the love that was petrified by liquor. It did not matter to me whether this was or was not the truth, since I knew that John had discovered some truth about himself and his ability to forgive by drawing his own conclusions about his father. His success was a lesson to us both; we understood that finding a reason to forgive had nothing to do with re-creating the past exactly as it was or pretending an allegiance to a high moral standard. We discovered that forgiving can be done for any reason at all; it is the act, not the reasoning, that matters.

18

Single Parents

Being raised in a home where there is only one parent often causes resentment against both the missing parent (usually the father) and the single parent (usually the mother). The reasons for single parenting are varied and complex: divorce, death, abandonment, or the desire of some individuals (predominantly women) to raise a child alone without a partner. Children of single parents normally expect their mother or father to be all things at once: mother, father, cook, housekeeper, and sports enthusiast—with an infinite supply of energy and compassion.

If the missing parent is deceased or unavailable, the anger that may arise toward that parent is deprived of a tangible object; the anger is detached and out of focus. On the other hand, if divorce is the reason for the separation, and the missing parent either lives alone or with a new family, the rage has an outlet, a real person on whom to lay both real and imagined blame. Separation is difficult for everyone involved, parents and children alike. Placing the blame on the parent who leaves home is always an easy, if unfair, solution. But the reverse is also true: many children blame one parent for driving the other one away. In both cases, it is a game without a winner, and living with blame hinders emotional stability as well as practical progress. It is impossible to reach maturity as an understanding individual if your childhood is spent looking for someone to blame.

Say to yourself:
Being a single parent is a very demanding job.
Searching for someone to take the
blame is a useless journey.

Compassion for the single parent can only surface if forgiveness is embraced and understood. Continuing to hold anger and resentment in our hearts toward a parent who had to be both mother and father will never allow us the chance to develop a compassionate response instead of an angry one. Forgiveness is the solution, since it is impossible to forgive without unlocking the door to compassion. If we can begin to understand the enormous difficulty of raising a child without the physical, financial, and emotional support of a spouse, then we can also begin to forgive what we may have seen as abuse or mismanagement.

Say out loud:
I cannot move forward if I keep
trying to rearrange the past.
Being the child of a single parent
is something I cannot change.

Try to imagine what it must have been like to raise a child alone. Think of the seemingly insurmountable difficulties that most single parents face each day. If your parent made a conscious decision to remain single, think of how important you must have been to that parent. If you were abandoned by one of your parents, focus on the one who remained and give him or her credit for having the courage to confront the obstacles imposed on a single person by chance and circumstance. Remember that you are not alone; there are millions of children who face life with only one parent. Reject the notion that you were somehow deprived, and recognize the fact that you cannot alter your personal history but you can change the way you perceive it. If your single parent did not do the kind of job you think you would have done, forgive that parent for whatever mistakes occurred.

Look in the mirror and say:
I will concentrate on the love I did receive,
not on what was missing.

Michael: A Profile

When Michael came home from school each day as a young boy, he went into the cellar and put on an old pair of high-heeled shoes that his mother had given him to wear whenever he got the urge. He would then climb the stairs and sit at the big oval table in the kitchen, eating cookies and milk with the shoes dangling from his too-small feet. Years later, when he was in high school, the shoes fit perfectly and complemented the dresses that his mother had altered to fit him. Michael's mother had been widowed while her son was an infant, and she loved the role that fate had awarded her. Prissy and overly feminine by nature, she had never been able to adjust to marriage and life in a house dominated by a man. She dressed her baby in delicate fabrics until he reached school age.

When Michael left his home in New England for New York City at the age of twenty, he brought along a few dresses to wear in the privacy of his new apartment. He never wore women's clothes out on the streets except for special occasions like Halloween or well-publicized drag balls held every few months for men who shared his fetish. The fact that there were others like him in the city made his love of dresses more acceptable, but his relationship with these men never went below the surface, and he missed having more intimate friendships.

Being very tall and sturdily built, Michael was offered a position on the basketball team in the office where he worked. He declined the invitation because he was ashamed of his inability to throw, bounce, or catch a ball. But with a little encouragement from a neighbor in his building, he began to practice at a local gym, and for the first time in his life he felt that his height was an advantage. On the day before he made the decision to join the office basketball team, he packed his dresses in a large shopping bag and put them on the street for collection. He kept this change of mind and habit as a secret from his mother for a long time. But by the time he was thirty years old, he had changed his appearance dramatically.

When he visited his mother on holidays, wearing sweatshirts, jeans, and sneakers, she tried to force him into wearing something "pretty" before he could sit down to dinner. If he mentioned his enjoyment of basketball, she would become agitated and change the subject. She mourned the loss of his long curls when Michael cut his hair very short, and was devastated by the news that he had thrown away her hand-stitched dresses and hand-me-down heels. During a particularly heated discussion one evening, she admitted to her son that she had prayed for a daughter and Michael's birth had come as a shock. She also admitted to never having loved his father very much nor being unduly upset when the man had passed away. She ended the discussion by telling Michael that her only regret in life was that he had not been a girl.

It took Michael many years to forgive his mother for her selfishness and lack of respect for his needs as a young man. During a short-lived sojourn in analysis, he admitted to himself that he had resented his father for dying so young and leaving him in the hands of a woman who refused to accept his masculinity. The bitterness he felt at being an outcast for most of his childhood and adolescence was intense and debilitating. Being in therapy only seemed to make matters worse; he hated the analyst for making him relive the pain. For several years he stopped visiting his mother even on major holidays, keeping in touch with an occasional phone call that always ended in anger. Forgiving his mother seemed an impossibility when we first discussed the idea, but in time he began to listen.

The first thing Michael was able to do was to stop blaming his father for dying; he finally saw the folly of such a belief and accepted the fact that his father had had no choice in the matter. Then gradually he began to understand his mother's neurotic need for a girl whom she could mold after herself. As irrational as this need must have been, he began to understand how disappointed his mother was to be saddled with a strong and sturdy boy.

Forgiveness did not bring about a reconciliation in Michael's case. On the rare visits to his aging mother's house he found that her happiness was dependent upon an outmoded illusion of femininity that threatened to suffocate the home in which he had been raised. He stopped going home altogether and filled his life with close friends, work, and basketball games. When his mother died, he sold her house exactly the way she had left it, and forgave himself for not wanting to keep any mementos.

19

Stepparents

Children of divorce often find one of their parents replaced by a relative stranger. This can also happen if there has been a death in the family or if a single parent decides to marry. Depending on the age of the child, dealing with an unknown figure of authority on familiar territory can be a monumental adjustment. Accepting a new member into an existing relationship takes time, patience, and a great deal of love if the merger is to be successful. If the new "parent" is not willing to understand a child's often hostile response, years of maladjustment may follow.

Adoptive parents are not stepparents in the strict sense of the word, but problems often arise when a child feels that he or she does not "belong," even if that feeling is erroneous. Again, age is a factor; if the adopted child is an infant the transition to a new family is often free of adjustment problems, even though some may surface later in life. In the majority of cases, adoptees look upon their stepparents, or foster parents, as their real family, regardless of blood ties.

As I stated in the preface, I accepted my new parents unequivocally and never had the desire to track down my biological family even though I had more information than most adoptees are accustomed to receiving. Being an infant when I was adopted helped, but I have known other adoptees with similar histories who felt "incomplete" unless they pursued their biological connection. For me, one set of parents was enough; I felt no compulsion to seek out and find another. I did, however, gather as much information about them as the adoption agency allowed, but even that did not prompt a further search. In my case, accepting my adoptive parents— including their shortcomings—as my own was something that occurred naturally. Based on my own experience, I tend to think that adopted children have difficulty with the concept of "belonging," but considering the reality of adoption, that sense of confusion seems normal in the sense that adjustments need to be made. Everyone— adopted or not—must learn to adjust to the intricacies of their childhood. I have always felt that giving up a child for adoption is a sacrifice based on compassion and love, at least in most cases. For a mother who is underage, unwed, economically deprived, or who may have a host of other problems to confront, finding a better home for her child is an act of tremendous courage.

This feeling of not belonging must be confronted by anyone involved in a situation where a biological connection is absent, such as when a new spouse enters the home after a divorce. The new member who joins an already existing family often feels that he or she does not really belong and has no right to give orders to a child that is not an offspring. The child often feels that the new addition is a threat to the stability of a family used to dealing with the absence of a mother or father. Adoptive parents have an easier time adjusting to the situation once the adoption is legal, but even they often have doubts about the nature of a bond that has no biological connection. Many children of adoptive parents find that as they mature they feel a need to discover their "natural" relatives, if they can find a way through the maze of laws that surround the circumstances of their birth records. This quest for their origin is usually not meant to hurt their adoptive parents: it is a need to satisfy curiosity or to fill what some adoptees regard as "blank spaces."

If you were raised by one or more parents not connected to you by genes, you may harbor resentment against them for valid reasons. Stepparents can and do abuse children in a variety of ways, and if the child knows that the abuse is coming from someone who is not related by blood, it makes the situation special. Men or women who marry a partner with children have to deal with their own feelings of inadequacy, belonging, and even jealousy. And they often have to do this in the face of steadfast resistance on the part of the children. Parents who adopt a child old enough to remember his or her past are often faced with the prospect of proving themselves and providing guidance with a combination of unquestionable love and sensitive discipline. Being either stepparents or stepchildren adds a potentially divisive ingredient to the already complicated matter of being an ideal family.

It is essential for all concerned to accept the reality

that ideal families are the stuff of imagination; they rarely, if ever, exist. All families have problems, and those that involve stepparents simply have a different dimension. There are no "normal" families any more than there are "ideal" families. Each family unit, like each individual, is unique.

Adopted children have to realize that their parents adopted them because they wanted to have children of their own and could not conceive. And stepchildren should be aware that the reason a new parent joined their family was because love was a factor. It is very rare indeed to find that the simple fact of stepparenting is the major cause of abuse. So if you are still hanging on to that notion as the reason for your distress, give it up and let it go. The reality of abuse does not depend upon a biological connection; it happens because real love and affection are missing or misguided. The old refrain of "You wouldn't do that if you were my real mother" does not hold water. "Real" mothers and fathers do all sorts of things they either regret or do not comprehend.

Say to yourself:
Biological connections do
not guarantee a trouble-free life.
I will move forward by letting go of
a past I cannot change.

The most common form of anger among stepchildren who grew up in a household where a new parent was introduced is the anger directed at the "real" parent for allowing someone new into the family unit. When this anger is combined with resentment for the "outsider," it becomes a prescription for a family in turmoil. Many divorced parents feel the need for adult companionship, or they simply fall in love again. The affection for the new spouse is separate and apart from their affection for their children, and it should not be confused by the reluctant offspring. Forgiving someone for falling in love again should be easy, but it often is not. Children want the complete attention of the parent they have come to rely on if divorce or death has caused a loss in the family. The introduction of a surrogate is perceived as a threat to that attention. And that is usually exactly what happens: the natural parent's attention becomes divided, although for a good reason. But in most cases this does not mean that love is withheld to a damaging degree. If it is, then real problems grow and thrive. If you are an adult who feels that you were cheated out of the love you deserved because it was given to a stepparent, it might be wise to reevaluate your own demands and consider forgiving both yourself, your natural parent, and your stepparent. By forgiving, you will erase the problem without negating the truth of what happened.

> **Look in a mirror and say:**
> **My perception of the past**
> **may be flawed.**
> **Forgiveness can change my perspective**
> **and free me from resentment.**

Eric: A Profile

When Eric was ten years old, his father and mother got a divorce, and two years later his mother remarried. Since the breakup had been relatively amicable, Eric got used to spending weekends and occasional nights during the week with his father. When his mother first informed

him that she was going to marry another man, Eric felt
betrayed and looked to his father for comfort. After the
marriage took place he began spending more and more
time in his father's house, and his mother reacted by
limiting his visiting schedule and forcing Eric to spend
more time with her and her new husband. The new rules
infuriated the boy, and he took his hostility out on both
his mother and his stepfather to such an extent that life
in the once-tranquil home became unbearable. He
begged his mother to let him live with his father, but she
adamantly refused his request. By the time he was
eighteen years old, his hatred had turned him into a
disturbed young man who left his mother's home and
moved to New York City.

No one escaped Eric's wrath: he blamed his father for
not intervening on his behalf, he vilified his mother as a
"whore," and he refused to speak to the man who had
come to take his father's place at the head of the table.
By cutting himself off from every member of his scat-
tered family, he hurt himself as much as he hurt them.
His refusal to forgive his mother for falling in love again
propelled him into a course of action that left him feeling
totally isolated from the parents he had once loved.

The only thing that stopped him from descending into
real oblivion was his love and talent for music. As young
as he was, he found a job with a small recording company
and worked his way into a position of authority before
the age of twenty-five. His coworkers considered him a
genius in his field, and offers to produce records poured
in faster than he could comply. With his reputation
assured and his finances in order, he felt as if he had
reached some kind of summit. But his refusal to forgive
his parents had left him constantly depressed and incapable of being alone. He lived with one woman after

another, fearful of any real commitment. When I first met Eric he was hooked on cocaine and pills and could not sit still for more than fifteen minutes at a time.

Over a period of five erratic and difficult years, he managed to wean himself away from the drugs that were in danger of destroying his career and reputation. A year later his father was transferred to the city by his company, and in time he and Eric became occasional dinner companions, if not friends. It took another two years before Eric was able to understand his father's reluctance to interfere with his ex-wife's decision to remarry. By carefully examining his own role in severing his family connections, Eric forgave his mother as well as his stepfather and himself. And in the long and arduous process, he taught me that even the most reluctant participant in a family disaster can change his mind and alter the path of negative thinking. His triumph was shared by everyone who knew him well enough to remember how angry he had once been, and his victory over resentment was a victory for us all.

20

Homosexual Parents

The discovery that one (or possibly both) of your parents is homosexual can be devastating unless that knowledge is imparted at a very early age. Even then, it involves tremendous adjustments and constant reassurance that sexual orientation does not alter parental love. More often than not, children discover this "hidden life" after they have passed the age of puberty or when divorce proceedings reveal the truth. All forms of parental sexual behavior are difficult for children to comprehend, but when homosexual orientation is admitted or exposed, the long-term effects are often monumental in scope and difficult to assimilate.

If you are an adult who resents a parent because his or her sexual preference is for members of the same sex, one way to release that resentment is through understanding the nature of forgiveness. Being able to forgive someone for something that is not their "fault" should be relatively simple, but that is not always the case, especially when it is a parent who is perceived as committing an unforgivable sin.

The first step is to understand that the human sexual response is not a choice; we choose our partners, to be sure, but we cannot control our preference for one gender over the other. Homosexuality is not a decision, it is a biological urge as strong as heterosexuality. Children of gay parents are often confused about the reasons for what they see as a deception. If one parent suddenly decides that he or she must come out of the closet and be true to his or her innermost sexual feelings, the question of why this did not happen sooner (before the marriage took place, for example) arises. Very little compassion is shown for the perceived "offender," who is finally able to reveal the truth in the face of possible rejection by all concerned. Making an admission of such possibly catastrophic dimensions is viewed as an admission of guilt rather than as a release. It is perfectly understandable that a child or adolescent may find such an admission confusing and troublesome, but to carry this childish response into adulthood is both selfish and self-destructive.

Homosexual parents are capable of giving and receiving love as much as "straight" parents are and, in many cases, even more so. A parent who has found the courage to acknowledge his or her sexuality in the face of such daunting odds against acceptance is a person who deserves respect, not resentment. Children of gay parents would be wise to overcome the irrational fears that society may impose, knowing that familial love is personal and does not require the approval of others to be valid. Forgiveness opens the door to acceptance and has the capacity to sustain the family against all odds, even if that family no longer functions as a unit under the same roof.

If one parent leaves the family home in order to begin a new life with another partner of the same sex, another dimension is added to the problem of divorce or separation. Accepting a parent's new lover or partner can be difficult, but it helps to remember that it is a choice, and rejection of the new lover is not automatically required. This question of choice also applies if living with a parent's new lover is part of the new arrangement of the household, even if cohabitation is only part-time. Children of gay parents are forced to make choices that most children of divorce are required to make, but accepting a stepparent of the same sex often makes that choice more difficult. Again, this is where the concept of forgiveness plays an important role in helping such assimilations occur without the specter of prolonged resentment. If real love and affection are present in the home, regardless of the sexual orientation of the heads of the household, adjustments can and must be made by all concerned in order to keep love alive.

Having a parent who is homosexual cannot readily be regarded as a form of parental abuse. Such a situation might be disruptive, to say the least, but it is not necessarily abusive. Falling in love with a member of the same sex has nothing to do with one's capacity to be a loving and caring parent. And children who choose to resent the reality of what has occurred are willing participants in a possible tragedy. If forgiveness is embraced in place of hostility, the resentment could be dissolved instead of carried into adulthood.

Remember: forgiveness, as well as resentment, are

choices to be made. Being human, we have the power to make decisions that affect our inner lives. And the possibilities that forgiveness offers are far more life-affirming than anything resentment has to offer.

William and Susan: A Profile

Born less than two years apart, William and Susan were unconventional siblings; they adored each other at first sight and their affection for each other grew stronger as they matured. Susan was the older of the two, and she treated her brother not as a rival but as a friend. By the time they were in high school, with William just one year behind his sister, they knew that their parents were on the verge of separation or divorce. This development, in what was once a close-knit family, came as a complete shock to everyone except their father, Fred, who had been trying for years to accept his own homosexuality.

The first sign of Fred's defection from the family came about by accident. Susan and William discovered their father coming out of a local bar with his arm around another man. William knew that the bar catered to the gay population of the city but kept this information to himself for some time, until Susan extracted it from him. After the incident they became aware that their father seemed to be drinking more than usual and was coming home later and later each night. Within six months, they knew that their parents' marriage was coming to an end, and they knew this before their mother did.

One year later, when Susan was about to graduate from high school and leave her brother behind as she entered college, Fred announced to his family that he was moving into an apartment of his own. No reasons for the move were given other than the need for a trial separation. He told his children that the time had come for him to discover who he really was, with no mention of sexuality. Since Susan was about to start a new life away from home, and William would follow in a year, Fred told his family that the time for such a change was propitious. One week after Susan's graduation, he left the family home for good.

During the summer that followed his move, Fred visited his family frequently, but every time he visited an argument erupted with either his wife or his son. Susan was his only sympathetic ally, and her refusal to question her father's move caused trouble between her and her brother for the first time in their lives. Fred offered very little information about his new life, but William and Susan were both convinced that he was exploring his newfound homosexuality.

On the last weekend in the summer, Fred announced that he would seek a divorce on the grounds of incompatibility. He also revealed that he would be sharing his life and his apartment with another man. William was disconsolate at the news, as was his mother, but Susan told her father that she understood his decision, adding that she had known several young men who were gay during her final year of school and that she liked and respected them for having the courage to tell her who they really were. She knew instinctively that her father had not ceased loving her, regardless of his expression of affection for another man. William disagreed, seeing his father's behavior as unacceptable and unforgivable.

William attended college in the heart of New York City, and after graduating he decided to settle there. His contacts with his father were almost nonexistent, other than the few hours spent together on major holidays after a determined push from Susan. By this time Fred had been through several short-lived relationships with other men before settling into one that seemed destined to thrive. Susan treated her father as she always had: with love and affection, even in the presence of her father's new lover. William showed nothing but disdain for the relationship and insisted on bringing his mother's name into the conversation whenever he visited his father's new home. He could not forgive his father for what he saw as a betrayal so great it had destroyed both his and his mother's life beyond repair.

By the time I met William, his father had been living openly as a homosexual for nearly a decade, and the concept of forgiveness had never entered William's consciousness. We discussed the possibility every time we met, but his resistance was stronger than his desire for change. He held on to his anger and resentment against his father with such force that even the persistence of his sister was not enough to alter his hostility. Susan knew that her father had not stopped loving his family simply because he was listening to his own heart, but she could not persuade her brother to acknowledge this. Seeing them together was a study in contrasts: two siblings with opposing views of the same father.

Many years later, I had the opportunity to spend some time with William. He had still not forgiven his father, and the resentment he felt was visible on his face. He told me that he understood the importance of choice, but he refused to change his mind. The anger that he felt consumed him to such a degree—and his guilt was so intense—that it was difficult to spend any length of time with him without feeling a sense of pity and loss. He spoke of his sister in derogatory terms as a means of showing his disapproval of her ability to forgive. Being in the presence of someone who has embraced resentment over forgiveness afforded me the chance to see hostility in action. It was not, and is not, a pleasant experience, even knowing that the possibility for change is never completely absent.

PART THREE

THIRTY LESSONS FOR THIRTY DAYS

21

Relaxation Techniques

Before beginning the lessons, take a few moments to put yourself into a relaxed state. The mind is far more receptive to new suggestions when you take the time to calm yourself and prepare your whole body to accept new information. If you try to do the lessons while you are nervous or in a hurry, your mind will be preoccupied and less responsive. Doing the lessons will not deplete your energy for the rest of the day; it may, in fact, enhance it.

Once you have chosen the spot you will use for your daily lessons, sit or lie down and make yourself comfortable. Place this book within easy reach with the lesson of the day accessible with a bookmark. Let your hands rest on your upper thighs, close your eyes, and concentrate on something that does not involve any action on your part except creating an image. A blank blackboard, white canvas, or a clear pool of water are possibilities, with water being an especially tranquil choice. As you focus your mind on the image, tell yourself that you will rest but not sleep, then take a few deep breaths before letting your lungs breathe normally.

Visualize your body from the top of your head to the tips of your toes, telling each section to relax in sequence like this:

My head and face are relaxed . . .

My neck and shoulders feel calm . . .

My arms are heavy . . .

My chest and stomach are breathing normally . . .

My buttocks are sinking into the chair (or couch) . . .

My legs are heavy and relaxed . . .

My entire body gently gives in to gravity . . .

I am completely relaxed and receptive . . .

When you feel relaxed and are conscious of your breathing, open the book to your lesson for the day and read it as many times as is necessary for you to memorize it. Then put the book aside and close your eyes again, repeating the lesson over and over until you feel that it is part of you. Be aware of how good it feels to be so completely relaxed. After a few minutes, tell yourself that when you open your eyes you will remember your lesson, be fully alert, and be filled with energy for the rest of the day. (When you do your nightly lesson before going to bed, tell yourself that you will remember the lesson and easily fall asleep.) Count slowly from one to five, knowing that when you reach five you will open your eyes and resume your regular activities.

22

Doing the Lessons

Once you have decided to do the lessons, it might be wise to start on the first day of the month; that way you will always be aware of what lesson you are doing on any given date, since each lesson takes a day. (Lesson One is done on the first of the month, Lesson Two on the second day, Lesson Three on the third, etc.) It is not essential to do this, and you may begin the lessons whenever you like so long as you limit yourself to one lesson per day. Promise yourself that once you begin the lessons, nothing will stop you from spending the ten or fifteen minutes a day required. If you know, for example, that you will be spending several days away from home during the coming month, plan to bring the book along and continue your lessons. If you cannot do that, pick another month when you are certain you can do the daily lessons one day at a time.

Planning ahead may be very useful; it will offer you the opportunity to make a conscious decision to change your life by releasing whatever resentment and anger you are harboring toward your parents. It also gives a structure to the process, and that will help you to complete the program. Since doing the lessons does not take an inordinate amount of time, you can still continue your daily routine without fear of being burdened by a time-consuming program. These lessons should not be viewed as a hindrance to the rest of your life; they should be seen as something to look forward to, as time spent on you and you alone.

Pick out the most comfortable spot in your home: a favorite chair or sofa, for example. You will be using the same spot every day for the next month to practice your lesson, and it is important to feel safe and secure. It is best to avoid using your bed unless you can prop yourself up with your head erect so that you will not fall asleep. The same is true for the sofa: do not lie flat. Do your lessons at approximately the same time every day if possible, once in the morning and once at night. Choose a time when you can be alone without any distractions. If it is absolutely impossible to find time alone in a very comfortable spot because of others in the home, then use whatever space you can find—the bathroom, the cellar, or a chair in the yard if the weather permits. Be aware that you can make any spot your own and feel safe, and remember that the most important thing is to not be disturbed for the few minutes it takes to do the lesson. Turn off all radios, televisions, or other appliances that make noise, and unplug the telephone.

When you are ready to begin, read your lesson for the

day. Do not read any other lesson, and never read the lesson that follows until the following day. One lesson is enough for anyone to memorize. You may say the lesson out loud or to yourself, whatever makes you comfortable. Once the lesson is in your mind, concentrate on it, but do not try to understand it completely if you feel confused. Keep breathing normally, and let the lesson wash over you like a soft, warm breeze. Spend about five minutes repeating the lesson and committing it to memory, then count to five and open your eyes.

Immediately following your morning lesson—once you have memorized it and opened your eyes—write the lesson down on a small piece of paper and put it in your pocket or purse so that you will have it with you for the rest of the day. Read the lesson to yourself every few hours during the day, or whenever you can find the time. Writing it down on paper in your own hand will help you to remember both the words and your commitment.

The first week's lessons are followed by a brief comment that is intended to help you absorb and understand the meaning of what you are committing to memory. Once you have finished the first week, there will be no further need for these comments; your mind will grasp the nature and meaning of the lesson with ease.

23

Sharing the Lessons

If you have a close friend who is also in the process of forgiving their parents by using this book, perhaps you can arrange to begin the lessons on the same day. That way you can discuss your feelings as the lessons progress. You must do the lessons alone, but having the opportunity to talk about how the lessons make you feel can add to the experience. If you choose this method, make certain that you choose a trusted friend who shares your concerns and your ultimate goal. Being able to talk about the changes you are making can be very beneficial so long as both parties are open to change. However, having a partner is by no means required, since this is a journey through your own personal history. If privacy is more important to you than sharing your feelings, then by all means do the program alone.

Remember: where you do the lessons is up to you, and the time you set aside is a gift to yourself. To accept that gift is a tribute to your willingness to make a change.

24

The Lessons Day by Day

LESSON 1

Starting today, I will stop letting the past intrude on the present.

It is not possible to live fully in the present if we allow our minds to be overly influenced by what happened to us in the past. We each have a personal history we cannot change, but we can change our minds about the present. Whatever mistakes we may have made in the past should not be allowed to intrude on today. This lesson will help you to let go of the past.

LESSON 2

Thinking about what happened in the past is a waste of time.

Spending time and effort thinking about what happened in the past will not help to clarify the present; it simply occupies our time and keeps us from moving forward. Learning from history is valuable, but so is living in the present without intrusion by the past.

LESSON 3

The past will no longer influence
my life in the present.

Living in the past stifles our lives and negates the immediacy of the present. By moving away from the past, we can direct our attention to today, and this will add needed strength to make positive changes.

LESSON 4

I cannot change the past, but I can change my mind about it.

No one has the power to rearrange the past; our personal histories are our own. But we can change and grow in spite of what occurred in the past, and by doing so, we can shift the focus on past events in a manner that alters their importance.

LESSON 5

I refuse to be a victim
of my past.

Being a victim of the past hinders growth in the present.
This lesson will help you to abandon the role of victim,
and by shedding that role you open yourself to new
choices.

LESSON 6

I am willing and able to let go of my past.

In order to truly leave the past behind, you first have to acknowledge that you have the capacity to make a positive move forward. Do this lesson (like all the others) even if you doubt your ability to integrate it into your life at this moment. Doing the lesson will help to reinforce your belief in your own capabilities.

```
LESSON 7

I am free of the constraints
of the past
and I now move forward.
```

We cannot move ahead if we are chained to the past. Being obsessed with the details of our formative years— or even with what happened last week—interferes with both present and future possibilities. This lesson leaves the past behind.

LESSON 8

**I cannot make positive changes
by criticizing myself.**

LESSON 9

**I would never allow another person
to criticize
me the way I criticize myself.**

LESSON 10

Constant self-criticism blocks my path toward self-approval.

LESSON 11

I am in the process of preparing myself for approval, not criticism.

LESSON 12

I do not deserve the kind of criticism I have given myself. I deserve something better.

LESSON 13

I will gently and easily replace self-criticism with self-approval.

LESSON 14

**I completely approve of who I am
and what I can become.**

LESSON 15

Blaming others for my problems is counterproductive.

LESSON 16

Blame is a negative emotion, and I choose to be positive.

LESSON 17

My parents are not to blame for my life in the present.

LESSON 18

By setting my parents free from blame, I free myself in the process.

LESSON 19

I take full responsibility for my life today.

LESSON 20

I no longer see myself as a victim of my parents' mistakes.

LESSON 21

I have changed my mind about being a victim and blaming my parents.

LESSON 22

I am not guilty of what I thought I was in the past.

LESSON 23

Guilt is a negative emotion, and I reject it from my life.

LESSON 24

I am willing to live in the present, free of blame and guilt.

LESSON 25

I am proud of myself for releasing my parents from blame and taking responsibility for my own life.

LESSON 26

I am preparing myself for a life of tolerance and understanding by giving up my need for blame, anger, and resentment.

LESSON 27

I forgive my parents for what they did and did not do.

LESSON 28

I forgive myself for what I did and did not do.

LESSON 29

Forgiveness feels better than anger and resentment.

LESSON 30

I will live my life one day at a time with forgiveness as my guide.

EPILOGUE

The purpose of the preceding pages has been to famil-
iarize you with the concept and practical application of
forgiveness, most specifically as it applies to you and
your parents. However, the process of forgiving can be
applied to anyone you know or have ever known. Anger
and resentment are not confined to parents only; we can
feel conflicting emotions toward our friends, lovers,
spouses, other family members, even strangers.

The overwhelming (and simple) reason to forgive is
that it makes us feel better. Forgiveness can be seen as
a nonjudgmental love that embraces tolerance and compassion. Forgiveness may involve a physical separation
from a family member or an old friend, but it also frees
both you and the person forgiven. Once you forgive
someone, hatred is erased, and you may find that there

is either no longer a place in your life for that person or that a lasting reconciliation has been effected.

Simple daily acts of forgiveness help to keep a relationship strong, but when a parent has been overly abusive or a spouse has been unfaithful, the act of forgiving may bring about dramatic changes in the alliance that no one can predict. If separation occurs, the act of forgiving will make the space between you easier to bear. And when the "mourning" period is over, the healing process will assure you that forgiveness repairs the *feeling* of separation, if not the physical reality. Give yourself some time to heal if you have experienced a loss in the process of forgiving, and remind yourself that you are free of the resentment that was undermining the quality of your life. Take credit for having the courage to rely on your ability to make a choice. No gods, gurus, or idols are required, since forgiveness is a prescription—written by you—for complete recovery. How you administer that prescription is your decision, but be aware that it often takes more than a single dose. By taking the medicine of forgiveness daily for a while, you will let this powerful and curative drug seep into your system to work its wonders. Think of it as a powerful vitamin that slowly and methodically heals your whole body by freeing it from the grip of resentment and fear.

In spite of the fact that the human species seems to be doing its best to destroy the world in which we live, that world itself, meaning Earth and the cosmos that surrounds it, is constantly in the process of creation. By repeating a cycle of birth and death with such mysterious beauty that it is impossible for us to comprehend it in its entirety, it often leaves us justifiably breathless and in awe. To see this cycle—which includes all life forms—as anything less than absolutely beautiful is to rearrange the universe in your own image of yourself, as if you had the power to step back and separate yourself from a world of unseverable ties, a world so interconnected that all of life can theoretically be traced back to one or more microscopic cells. If you see the natural world as ugly, you are simply seeing yourself distorted, you are not seeing the entire picture accurately, you are not seeing what may be the only absolute truth.

Because we are individuals, each of us unique in his or her own way, the notion of being separate and apart appears to be valid. But such beliefs are inventions of the ego and have nothing to do with actual fact. Being an individual means being a part of the whole; a vast collection of cells that contribute to the molecular makeup of the cosmos. The cells of humans are evolved replicas of the cells of all living things; we have far more in common than our physical differences might indicate.

By understanding and acknowledging the interconnectedness of all living things, as well as our relationship to the rest of the cosmos, we are allowed the opportunity to see our parents as reflections of ourselves, as individuals who share both a familial connection and a cosmic one as well. This change in perception is often enough to make the concept of forgiving that much easier to consider. Getting stuck in the rut of seeing our parents as nothing more than familial authority figures negates their rightful place in the scheme of things, as members of the world community. By seeing them as integrated, rather than separate, it may be easier to forgive their faults. Being human, we need all the help we can get in order to change our minds about who our parents really are, regardless of the role they played in our lives. Making a change means making a choice, and seeing our parents in a different light is essential.

Do not, however, be discouraged if you have difficulty forgiving someone who has hurt you so terribly that the wound seems beyond healing. The act of forgiving shines a light through the darkest and most impenetrable clouds. Once you begin the path to forgiveness it is difficult to fail; if you think you have, you can always try again. Give yourself as much time as you need, and try to remember that you are not in competition with anyone; you are doing this for yourself.

If you have read this book in its entirety, done the lessons as prescribed, and still feel resentment against your parents, do not consider yourself a failure. This process may not work for everyone who studies these pages. But before you dismiss the concept of forgiveness as unworkable for you, try one brief and final exercise.

Get two pieces of blank paper and write the following words on one sheet in bold letters:

ANGER   FEAR   RESENTMENT

On the other sheet of paper, write these words:

TOLERANCE   LOVE   FORGIVENESS

Look at the two sheets of paper and tell yourself that you can destroy only one of them. The choice is yours. Take your pick.

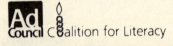